M000086949

Through the Eyes of Love

By Crystal Owens

Scriptures marked KJV are taken from the KING JAMES VERSION (KJV): KING JAMES VERSION, public domain.

Copyright © 2019 THROUGH THE EYES OF LOVE

All rights reserved— Crystal Owens

No part of this book may be reproduced or transmitted in any form or by any means, graphic, electronic, or mechanical, including photocopying, recording, taping, or by an information storage retrieval system without the written permission of the publisher.

B.O.Y. Publications, Inc.
P.O. Box 1012
Lowell, NC 28098
www.alwaysbetonyourself.com

Cover and Interior Design: B.O.Y. Enterprises, Inc.
Author Photo: HB Photography

Printed in the United States.

ISBN: 978-1-7338051-3-1

Acknowledgements

I would like to first thank Jesus Christ, my Lord and Savior, for His unconditional love! For teaching me to love others as He loves me, helping me to see that He never gives up on me. So, in return I cannot give up on others, regardless of who they are, how they live, or what they have done. I give ALL glory to Him in all things, and for this blessed opportunity to share a glimpse how His magnificent love can overcome ANY circumstance. It was His strength, mercy, and grace that got me through these darkest times of my life. It was God that lead me to the writing of this book, to the opportunity by divine appointment to get it published, and He provided me with all the resources in which to get it done. I also credit to Him every person changed, and every relationship restored. I give God all the glory! He is so worthy!

Second, I would like to thank my husband, Tracy Owens, for believing in me and loving me enough to stand with me through the whole process, not to mention through the dark times written in this book. I could of never have went through all this without your love and support. You are my backbone, and I thank God for you!

I would like to say to our children: Morgan (Hannah) I love you and no matter what, I am and always will be proud of you, because I KNOW you, and am grateful God is restoring you and making you into the beautiful young woman He has created you to be!   Brian (Bryson), Ashley, and Taylor and our granddaughters, Emma and Kendell, I love you all! So proud of all of our children and love you guys with all of my heart! Regardless of what you do, I want you to know my love never changes for you! I pray salvation, blessings, and prosperity, and much LOVE to all of you!

Table of Contents

INTRODUCTION

What is the first thought that comes to mind when you hear the word "love?"

In a world where the word is so often used, yet most of the time, with no real meaning, having no understanding, there is no depth and no ground to stand on. I've been told so many times "Love never fails" and as I walked this journey called "life," I often wondered how they come up with this concept. It's been said, the older you get, the wiser you get. Yet, when it comes to the subject of love and it never failing, I sure wasn't getting any wiser. It seemed like the older I got the less love seemed to appeal to me, despite my attempts to see it win a battle over the wounds inflicted from past. It wasn't until some critical life changing events in my life that I began to learn the true meaning of love. I had an encounter with not only a love that never fails but love HIMSELF! Being saved for many years, my understanding of love changed. What I knew as love turned out to be conditional and about satisfying me, not others. In this encounter, I learned to walk out a love that was about the other person, yet was so amazing, it made me free in the process. It gave me a new outlook on others, and through it all, I gained understanding along with an intimate relationship with God. This relationship grew to be much more than just knowing about Him. Now I know that He doesn't just possess love, He IS love! Love is the very essence and heart of God! I have truly experienced the HEART of God!

So, as this world becomes more evil and wickedness seems to lurk for those who are weak, weary, and wounded; I pray this book brings healing and deliverance to the brokenhearted. I pray for those who are bound and in captivity to be made free as you walk your own experience *Through the Eyes of Love*!

Chapter 1

What's love got to do with it?

Many times, I've heard the sermons preached about how Jesus died on the cross for our sins. The gruesome pictures depicted in my mind, and to hear the echo of the words in my head "CRUCIFY HIM! CRUCIFY HIM!" would ring in my ears. This seemed to have been the most cataclysmic event EVER to have taken place in history, as heaven and earth collided and the war between good and evil was at its climatic height in the spirit realm where the fight for mankind was battled!

I can only imagine the immense magnetic force of fear in the atmosphere that day. As the orders were carried out by the Roman soldiers, those who walked closely with Jesus watched what seemed to be their only chance at hope die right in front of their very eyes. The constant tugging of fear gripping at their minds had to be telling them they would be next. Jesus had been trying to prepare them for what was to come. But, for years they'd experienced the miracles, teachings and personal meetings with the master teacher himself. Though He'd explained parables and performed great wonders, those experiences were not enough to keep the fear from gripping them to the point of denying him, running and hiding from the very thing Jesus had tried to warn them about for years. As I began to focus on this whole scenario of Jesus' death and the indescribable torture that he endured, I asked the Lord many times, "What's LOVE got to do with this?" because it sure brought negative feelings to my mind. I felt sadness, guilt, condemnation, and confusion! I often asked the Lord questions that seemed farfetched like, "Did I REALLY take part in this?" "HOW? WHEN I WASN'T THERE, I WASN'T EVEN BORN! Lord, I couldn't be so heartless to commit such a terrible act to another human being, especially not you Lord!"

In my search for answers, I never realized I was being blinded by the enemy in his attempts to keep me from reaching my God-given purpose. I couldn't seem to put together the relation of the cross, the unimaginable beatings, and God's love. How could dying in such grotesque way have ANYTHING to do with love? I couldn't wrap my head around all this. Why is the cross so significant? What makes God's love so special or different than what I've ever known love as before? Why does God love us so much? The more I thought about it, the more questions that came to mind. Yet, without answers, I became frustrated and started to ignore all the questions. As I heard it said all my life, we're not supposed to question God. He has reasons for everything, and He is a sovereign God. We are to just accept it as it is, so I just BELIEVED He loved us and died for us, but never understood why. The first scripture I ever memorized was the one that most people, even a lot of sinners, know today.

"For God so loved the world, that he gave his only begotten Son, that whosoever believeth in him should not perish, but have everlasting life." -John 3:16 KJV

I am not one who is satisfied with just knowing *about* something. I am a very inquisitive thinker. My mom tells me I think too deep sometimes, so… I thought about that! With so many questions left unanswered, I began to wonder, "How can I believe in something that I don't even understand?" That would be like being with your spouse and not knowing them at all. It is a taught knowledge with no real connection to link you together, like the vows without the commitment. A true commitment is a heart issue, it's a decision, a made-up mind, not a feeling, and where there is no commitment, it's much easier to just let go when the storms of life come rolling in without warning! It's not a good thing to be ruled by emotions and feelings because we would never have stability. We would be as the disciples were, ruled by the feeling of fear, therefore unable to stand in the boldness that Jesus has given us the authority to walk in.

God knew I was searching for answers that I would so desperately need years later in my life… answers that, had I kept ignoring, would have brought devastation to me spiritually and emotionally. He led me to a passage of scripture in the 3rd chapter of Ephesians that let me know that it *is* for me to **know** His love at an intimate level, not just a mere mental assent.

"That he would grant you, according to the riches of his glory, to be strengthened with might by his Spirit in the inner man; That

Christ may dwell in your hearts by faith; that ye, being rooted and grounded in love, May be able to comprehend with all saints what is the breadth, the length, and depth, and height; And to know the love of Christ, which passeth knowledge, that ye might be filled with all the fulness of God. Now unto him that is able to do exceeding abundantly above all that we ask or think, according to the power that worketh in us, Unto him be glory in the church by Christ Jesus throughout all ages, world without end. Amen. **Ephesians 3:16-21 KJV**

I began to read this passage frequently and pray for the Lord to show me what the breadth, the length, the depth, and the height of Christ love was. I began to meditate on these scriptures and started seeing that it is God's desire for us to know Him at an intimate level. I was hungry to know more about His love! It was then that He began to lead me to the cross on several different occasions. Despite the many years of being a Christian, since my early teens, I had intentionally ignored the cross, because of a sense of sadness and guilt. Due to my lack of understanding, the very thought of the whole ordeal just really bothered me. But God begin to put me on the path, that would eventually reveal to me the true meaning and revelation of the cross.

Three main situations come to mind where God placed me in those paths. Our church had an Easter play one year in which I was asked to play a part. It consisted of the manger scene, the cross, and the tomb, which one person was placed at each scene. Of course, they placed me at the cross even though I wasn't really sure about this role. They gave us a script to go by, but told us that we were free to add to the script or change it if we would like as long as it was in sync with the bible text. Being really excited about my role, I wanted the Lord to use me to touch people through the part I was playing. I went home and looked at the script that was given for me to go by and then began to get into the scriptures in the bible. I prayed and asked God to help me present my part just like He wanted me to, and He did! The play went great! The alter was full at the end of the play! This began to spark something within me, but I still wasn't at all clear as to the meaning or significance of the cross.

Several years later, I ran into another situation that caused me to look at the cross. My mom, a friend of ours, and I attended a 3-day Christian conference where the presence of the Lord was so strong it was tangible! As I was listening to the word brought forth by the speaker, all of a sudden, this lady in front of me seemed to become extremely annoying to my ears! I suddenly was being so distracted by her "Amen" and "Praise God" that I was missing the word that was being released! I had become so irritated that I couldn't hear anything the speaker was saying. All I could focus on was this annoying voice, not realizing that it was a spirit of distraction trying to block me from receiving what the Lord was giving to me! I didn't rebuke it or take authority over it. I allowed it to steal part of the word from me. Finally, they took a break for lunch and boy did I need a break! As soon as I got in the car, I asked them, "Is that lady sitting in front of us getting on your nerves?"

They both replied, "What woman?"

I said, "What do you mean, WHAT WOMAN? The one in front of us that is louder than the speaker, that yells every two minutes Praise the Lord, and Amen!"

My mom replied, " I hear her but it's not distracting me, she's just excited about the word preached. It must be the devil distracting you so you don't receive the word."

We got back to the conference after break, and I told my mom and friend that if that lady was sitting in front of us, I was moving to another seat! We got back to our seats, and I didn't see that lady in front of us, but her husband was sitting there, so I knew that she was going to be sitting there again. I could feel the heat rising up me already and hadn't even seen her yet! This lady had no idea that I was so irritated at her, but God did. I thought maybe she had gone to the restroom since she wasn't there in her seat, when all the sudden I felt a tap on my shoulder, and it was her! She handed me a book, and said, "The Lord told me to buy this for you." The name of the book was *The Cross... The Epicenter of Glory* by Mahesh Chavda. I felt like I was melting! Tears welled up in my eyes and I hugged her and said, "Thank You!"

That irritation left me, and I was able to hear and receive from the word preached. Then, when we got into the car, we were talking about what happened, and I said, "I didn't want that book. I wanted another book! I should have known it would be about the cross again!"

My mom said, "Well that's too bad! You may not have wanted that one but if God told her to buy it for you, then that is the one you needed! He knows what you need when you don't."

It seemed like I still wasn't getting it. He was leading me to the cross over and over, but why? Shortly after this, I had a third and very different experience that would change my view of the cross forever! It began one rainy morning on my way out to crank my car. I had on a pair of old but very comfortable flip flops. I went to step down on our back porch steps and my left foot slipped out from under me, causing me to fall and break my left ankle. A few days later, my husband received a phone call, informing him they were calling the family in for his uncle, who had cancer in Florida. My husband and I were going to go with his parents to Florida, but I was unable to go due to an orthopedic appointment for my ankle to be set. I was out of work at this time, until the doctor released me. When they left for Florida, I told the Lord I was going to use this time to spend with Him. I really enjoyed that time reading the bible, praying, and singing to the Lord. About the third day into this, I heard the Lord say, "Build a cross."

I repeated it back to Him, "Build a cross? Why?"

He didn't answer me back, but I *knew* it was the Lord, NO DOUBT IN MY MIND! So, I immediately started searching scriptures about the cross. I could not for the life of me understand *WHY* He wanted me to build this. Later, that evening my husband called me and while we were talking, I said, "The Lord said to build a cross." My husband didn't seem shocked or puzzled, his only question was, "How big?" I wasn't expecting that at all. I said, "I don't know, I'll give you all the details when you get back home." After returning from his trip, my husband got started on the cross. I was at work, when he sent me a picture of a cross approximately 7 ft. tall. He also had built a small seat/alter in front of it in the woods. When I saw the picture, I just began to cry because I didn't have to beg or plead with him. I actually forgot about it and didn't even have to remind him. Wow! How it blessed me!

The next morning, I arose early and went down to the cross while the sun was barely beginning to peek through the trees. I began to talk to the Lord and asked Him, "Ok, Lord, why did you want me to build this cross? What are you trying to tell me? And why have you led me to the cross on several occasions?" For several days I did this with no answer, no response, but went anyway. There was an internal pull drawing me, causing me to go early in the morning and some evenings. I just couldn't stay away. I would sit down on the ground and lean on the seat/alter, or sometimes sit on the seat, and just ponder, what is so special about this? I always took my bible with me to read and pray and meditate. After few days of this I was sitting at the foot of the cross and became very sleepy, so I laid my head down on the seat, and dozed off for what seemed like few minutes. I'm not exactly sure how long it was, but I was awakened by a bright beam of light from the sun shining through the trees right on the cross. It looked like a picture you would see in a movie, but much more beautiful! As I was waking up, I heard the Lord say, "This is the symbol of my love!" The revelation of this truth seemed to have melted my heart, as an overwhelming warmth began to cover me from head to toe, as if someone had poured very warm wax over my head until I was saturated entirely! It was the most wonderful feeling I ever felt, so much so, that I can barely find the words to describe it! With the sun rays shining and the voice of God speaking, it was as if I began to melt inside. I began to sob uncontrollably! At that very moment, I **KNEW!** It was becoming real to me! As I was crying, I looked up at the cross again and I saw a vision of Jesus hanging on the cross, the vision that for many years had disturbed me, and this time I heard Jesus say,

> *"Father, forgive them; for they know not what they do."*
> **Luke 23:34 KJV**

He then led me to this scripture for deeper understanding,

> *"Greater love hath no man than this, that a man lay down his life for his friends."* **John 15:13 KJV**

I could see the relation of the death on the cross with His love through this revelation. In that moment it was very clear as to why the enemy had deceived me for so many years to keep me from experiencing the freedom of what Jesus bought for me through God's love, the agape love of God! We all hope God loves us, but do we truly believe He does? And with what conditions? When we do something wrong, we begin to question His love for us, based on circumstances and the way we live our lives. But, He said in this passage of scripture that Christ died for the ungodly.

"And hope maketh not ashamed; because the love of God is shed abroad in our hearts by the Holy Ghost which is given unto us. For when we were yet without strength, in due time Christ died for the ungodly. For scarcely for a righteous man will one die: yet peradventure for a good man some would even dare to die. But God commendeth his love toward us, in that, while we were yet sinners, Christ died for us." **Romans 5:5-8 KJV**

This passage goes far beyond the righteous, even the good man, but goes as far as the sinner and the ungodly. To define ungodly according to KJV dictionary, it states 1.) wickedness 2.) impiety 3.) neglecting the fear and worship of God or violating His commands 4.) sinful; ungodly deeds. Soon after I received this revelation of God's unconditional love, and it became real to me. I began walking through trials that would definitely cause me to begin developing this same love He has placed within me.

Chapter 2

A Loving Example

Still trying to grasp this agape kind of love that was lingering in my head, I began to meditate on God's love to get a clearer understanding. I began to think back, from an early part of my life even until now, I've always had a heart for people. I've always had this drawing within me that seems to want to reach out to help those in need. Whether within or beyond my abilities, I do my best to help others… whether it's a physical need, financial help, lending a helping hand, even just an encouraging word. When I met people who seemed hopeless, I thought, this was how we do life. We reach out and bless others as God has blessed us. This eventually leading me to my current career as a nurse. I say this with much respect for nurses, but just because we carry a license with a title tagged to it, does not make us a nurse. Many people carry a title on their badges but don't have the true desire to fully carry out the intended roles. I began to think of the true nursing role model. Florence Nightingale came to mind as I would meditate on God's love and I would begin to relate to God's love through nursing. Florence Nightingale was the founder of nursing. She had a heart of compassion to nurse wounded soldiers in the Crimean War back to health while showing love and comfort. She believed that if the physical pain was present, the ability to comfort them would help lessen the intensity of suffering. She also was a strategist.

She began to log and make diagrams as to the death of soldiers and found out that most soldiers didn't die from their wounds, but a much higher rate was because of the unsanitary environments they were in. Thus, most died from infections, which was secondary to the wounds. She stepped outside of her comfort zone, with courage and boldness. Being a woman taking care of men in the hospital in that time was not permitted. Therefore, she had to press her way through the Generals just to be able to do small task such as giving them drinks to hydrate them or strengthen them with warm herbal drinks. She did all she could to help. Her compassionate heart drove her to go beyond what was allowed in that dispensation for women, because she desired to help those who were dying from sicknesses, that mostly could have been prevented. After writing several letters to the Generals with her findings, they allowed her to take a group of nurses into these extremely dirty hospitals, and they began to clean those areas. They provided beds for the men to be comfortable, as they had previously laid on the hard floors. They were also able to push for clean supplies to change the bandages to the physical wounds, thus decreasing germs and bacteria which cause infections as well. Florence Nightingale, then became known as the Lady with the Lamp, as she would make rounds to check on every wounded soldier in the hospital in the late-night hours and make sure they were comfortable.

Nursing is far more than a job, or career. It is far more than a way of living. The role of a nurse/patient advocate follows a far deeper meaning than all those things. The *TRUE* nursing role is not self-centered at all. Nursing should always be patient centered, focused on physical and emotional needs, and often includes the families. Our goal should always plan for the best outcome possible while providing them with the treatments and encouragement needed to aide them back to health, while always assessing and observing underlying issues that may contribute to hindering the healing process. The Lord also showed me, there are more people in need of emotional healing these days than there are people in need of physical healing. People are hurting spiritually and emotionally, as well as physically. Pain that is within is a heart issue, which is often times a bitter root of unforgiveness. This can lead to physical damage to the actual body through manifesting diseases or illnesses worsening. The bible shows some of this in scripture.

"A sound heart is the life of the flesh: but envy the rottenness of the bones." **Proverbs 14:30 KJV**

Envy in this passage of scripture refers to jealousy, bitterness, resentment and discontentment. The definition for the word rottenness is suffering from decay, which means leaving these issues unresolved or not dealt with, leads to physical damage to the body.

We use nursing assessments as a fundamental tool to help us evaluate a patient's physical, mental, and emotional state. They also give us a baseline as to what and where to start our process of elimination. I continually think on how nursing relates to the love of God and see so many aspects of how His love and nursing are both multi-dimensional. They are not superficial or one dimensional. They are not self-centered. They both are always in giving mode, focus on the healing process, and always bring comfort and compassion to those who are in need. This reminds me of a scripture that always catches my attention, when Jesus said,

> *"The Spirit of the Lord is upon me, because he hath anointed me to preach the gospel to the poor; he hath sent me to heal the broken-hearted, to preach deliverance to the captives, and recovering of sight to the blind, to set at liberty them that are bruised, To preach the acceptable year of the Lord."* **Luke 4:18, 19 KJV**

The anointing placed on him was heart driven, compassion to see those who were wounded and bound made free. This is the love of God. Love is the driving force of compassion. Only love can drive someone past their own desires to aide another person. Love is also referred in the King James Version and other references as "charity". Charity is defined as the voluntary giving of help, to those in need. In scripture, charity is the agape kind of love which is God's love, the highest form of love as described in *1 Corinthians 13:4-8:*

> *"Charity suffereth long, and is kind; charity envieth not; charity vaunteth not itself, and is not puffed up, Doth not behave itself unseemly, seeketh not her own, is not easily provoked, thinketh no evil; Rejoiceth not in iniquity, but rejoiceth in the truth; Beareth all things, believeth all things, hopeth all things, endureth all things. Charity never faileth..."*

Love being described as charity, as seen in scriptures above, is never self-seeking. The passion of love is in the heart of giving itself to fulfill the needs and desires of another, to bless another without requiring back from the one in which it was received. The only way love is able to function is to give it away. Love by itself is useless, and kept to oneself often leads to perversion, which is lust. Lust is always self-seeking, as we see in the world today. Love on the other hand, is an energetic force of giving, and works no other way. It's the most powerful force against all evil! Nothing can stop it, and IT NEVER FAILS! It is purpose driven. God is always giving to us through His love, and He commands us to love as we have been created in His image after His likeness. (Genesis 1:26) In that we are Christians, we are to love like He loved, all of mankind; good, bad, evil, and indifferent.

In scripture, Jesus gave commandment to *love the Lord thy God with all thy heart, and with all thy soul, and strength, and with all thy mind,* and to *love thy neighbor as thyself.* **Matthew 22:37-40, and Mark 12:30-31, Luke 10:28 KJV**

There is no division in these passages of scripture. If we are going to make a difference in this world today, we are going to have to get back to the *ONE* commandment that was given to us and the VERY source in which we were reconciled back to God through Jesus Christ...Love! His blood was shed for our sins and to reconcile us back to the Father, BECAUSE HE LOVES US! His love is driven by passion and purposed to help others who aren't able to help themselves. YES! No doubt, it was very painful for Jesus to bear the weight of our sins, but love compelled Him to give His life so that we wouldn't have to bear the weight of sin and can have and live life abundantly. Today, we see so many self-seekers, people who are focused on receiving love, but never giving love back. Therefore, it has been perverted into a lust form; envy, jealousy, and hatred, because it feels as if it deserves something, which is all self-centered. But love being exchanged from one to the other, brings joy, peace, and happiness.

Hereby perceive we the love of God, because he laid down his life for us: and we ought to lay down our lives for the brethren. But whoso hath this world's good, and seeth his brother have need, and shutteth up his bowels of compassion from him, how dwelleth the love of God in him? My little children, let us not love in word, neither in tongue; but in deed and in truth. And hereby we know that we are of the truth, and shall assure our hearts before him. For if our heart condemn us, God is greater than our heart, and knoweth all things. Beloved, if our heart condemn us not, then we have confidence toward God. And whatsoever we ask, we receive of him, because we keep his commandments, and do those things that are pleasing in his sight. And this is his commandment, That we should believe on the name of his Son Jesus Christ, and love one another, as he gave commandment. **1 John 3:16-23 KJV**

Chapter 3

Love Misunderstood

As a child, my perception of love was one dimension, as I only knew the kind of love that a child experiences through family and friends. Growing up with my paternal grandparents, my dad, Richard, two sisters (at the time), and my aunt, we were a very close-knit family. My aunt and cousins would come over practically every day. It seemed like they lived with us most of the time, but we were just close. My mom, Doris, would come and get us on weekends so we could spend time with her and my other siblings. My dad and mom divorced when I was around one year old, but I never thought I was affected by that separation, being that I was so young. There is no doubt that, in their differences, they both loved me and my sisters dearly. I never once felt that I was part of their problem. I don't remember them fussing or any of the details that lead up to their decision to divorce, so most of the memories of my childhood are good. Life was good. At that time in life, there were no video games or cell phones to distract us from each other. We played outside together, watched TV programs together, went to church together, ate meals together at the table, and fussed with each other. But we also took up for each other when others were messing with one of us. We had love shown to us by our grandparents, our dad, our mom, and each other. We were taught to share with one another and respect one another otherwise our dad would make us hug each other and say I love you or I'm sorry, and boy we hated that! But now I cherish that, seeing the lack of love and respect I see in many children and families now. I realize it was not as much to punish us, but it was to teach us the importance of respect and family relation-ship.

As I grew older, around 12 years old, my dad started dating a lady, which became pretty serious and we moved from South Carolina to North Carolina. They seemed to be in love. She was very nice to me and my sisters, like a second mom. I never once remember her mistreating us. She had no children of her own. They dated several years and were even engaged to get married but eventually broke up. I never really found out why, I never saw them fuss or argue to that degree. Despite the break-up, we stayed in North Carolina, since dad had a job and we were in school and pretty much settled at that point.

Later, I experienced my own broken relationship. After gradu-ating high school, I married a man named Mark and eventually had two children, a daughter we named Hannah, and a son we named Bryson. I also found myself in a divorce after an 18-year relationship. It was devastating at first, as that was the only se-rious and intimate relationship I ever knew. I thought it would last forever, based on the moments we shared while young, wild, and free. Eventually, our interests began to change, and our desires were no longer the same as we began to slowly drift apart over the years. As we began to explore our own adven-tures in life, we no longer had the same perception of life and what we wanted long term. These differences brought wounds into our marriage. Through so much hurt and pain, we became toxic, not realizing the damage we'd caused to ourselves and each other. Never thinking how it would affect us, much less the damage it would bring to our children.

I dealt with a lot pain from what seemed like half of my heart being ripped out of me, because I truly believed once I married it would be forever. I took my vows very seriously. I had feelings of guilt and confusion about the right and wrongs of marriage. I agonized over whether to go back and try again because I genuinely wanted to do what I thought was right. However, after giving my all and praying for years, it seemed like things were getting worse. The decision to continue exposing my children to our toxic behaviors or getting them to what I thought would bring them peace was so overwhelming. I cried out and asked God, "Lord, if it's really over, PLEASE take the love for him out of my heart!" It seemed like almost instantly, the pain left! I realized at that moment that it wasn't the love that was hurting me, but the pain of disappointment and failure. I was also hurt by the fear of the unknown because the marriage was all I ever knew. As divorce is never God's will, I began to pray and ask God questions like how and why? I began to see that the choice for us being together was a choice that we made ourselves, not God. Mark and I never sought God about who He had prepared for us in marriage. I began to see it was a decision we made in the flesh, without the understanding of true commitment. We thought we knew what was right. We loved each other to the degree that we understood love.

However, being so young, we had very limited knowledge of what true love was. We thought the fluttering feeling of puppy love that we were experiencing would be strong enough to stand the tests of times and carry us to the end of life together. We never realized that kind of love was sensual and had no foundation to stand on. With the lack of understanding, we were only committed as far as we understood love. Each time adversity came, it brought more anger, resentment, and division until it finally destroyed our marriage.

Soon after the separation, bitterness and hurt began to surface. We both had our share of "getting back" at one another. I began to say, "I'm free for the first time since I was 15 years old. I don't have to answer to anybody anymore!" I had convinced myself I was going to live life for me now! I began to dress up and wear makeup again and started going to a local bar and dance club. I started hanging out with old friends and drinking, which was the very thing I hated Mark doing while we were married because of the damage and pain it caused to me, our children, and eventually our marriage. I thought I was happy as the alcohol gave me a good feeling at first. While I was drinking it seemed as though I was having so much fun. While during this time, Mark began exhibiting behaviors of bitterness and hurt as well. He made false reports of communicating threats, saying that a mutual male friend of ours, Trey, was communicating threats to him via telephone. This was done out of jealousy and spite because he thought Trey and I were seeing each other even though at the time we were only friends, nothing more. Although he had a girlfriend that he brought to court with him multiple times, trying to get under my skin. As time progressed, Mark became more entertained with his new lifestyle and things got a little quieter between us. We still were not able to hold a conversation or speak to one another at a mature level concerning our children or any other issue because the bitter pain and hurt that were left unresolved, always seemed to resurface. As days and months went by, I began to drink more, thinking I was enjoying life. Trey and I eventually began dating. We were accused of it when nothing was going on so I said, well they accuse us, we might as well, just to really give them something to talk about. I started giving less attention to my own responsibilities, my children. I had become so consumed with what made me happy, or so I thought, while also trying to find out how to live on my own for the first time ever with two pre-teens. Hannah was 14 and Bryson was 12 at the time of our separation, and they were experiencing their own pain and hurt from a newly broken family. I realize, upon this writing, that the children were both very quiet during this major shift in our lives, as they didn't want to cause anymore drama between their dad and me. They were never given the opportunity to express how it was affecting them. Honestly, I don't even know if I thought about how it was affecting their lives at the time. As they were pulled into the vacuum of our bitter and negative emotions, a lot of the emotional stress was placed on them. I didn't see it then, but it is clear now. They were too young and inexperienced to understand how to release the stress that they were placed under, so they bottled it in for a while. I was there for them physically and financially, but I have to admit I wasn't there emotionally to support them, as I was developing my own coping skills and strategies with moving forward. I really take a lot of blame now as I look back at the situation. It breaks my heart because moms and dads get hurt, thus trying to heal themselves however they find comfort. This ultimately leaves the children prey to the world to teach them. While we, as parents, are blinded with our "self" motives and desires. We forget that the children need more love and attention during this time because they didn't ask for this! They didn't choose this life. They get confused, and sometimes afraid to say or express themselves because they feel like they are pulled between the two parents. I really struggled with that and no one really knew, but I couldn't change it after the fact, so I eventually had to learn to give them to God and let Him fix the kinks that me and their dad caused.

Not long after reality settled in, things begin to quiet down between Mark and I, but I began seeing changes in my children's attitudes and behaviors, mostly in their schoolwork and performances. Bryson had experienced a lot of anxiety and fear during his younger years, due to the fact that he was exposed to so many traumatic situations while Mark and I were together. He had always been my quiet child who removed himself from chaotic situations. He is still to this day fairly quiet around most people. Hannah was a black belt in karate, and almost having her second-degree black belt, she began missing classes to hang out with friends, then eventually quit karate. She began having a lot of issues in high school with other girls, arguments, suspended from school for fighting, in school detention multiples times for bad behavior, and skipping school and classes all together. She quit high school toward the end of eleventh grade. This beautiful, blonde hair, blue eyed girl was so outgoing, and very smart, with her whole life ahead of her. She could be anything she chose to become, with no doubt. She had a personality that was so bubbly, and truly could steal any person's heart. Her smile was so radiant that it drew attention of people from all around her, and yes, a lot of boys. This caused jealousy to become a huge problem which is why she was in a lot of confrontations in school. As time passed, she was constantly seeking the attention, love, and acceptance that she felt she was stripped of through the divorce. She mainly wanted the love of her daddy, Mark. She went to all lengths to get the love and attention she was searching for, but the void was still there. The harder she went after it, the more tangled in the traps of this world she became. Mark had gotten into drugs not long after the divorce, and over a period of time went to prison for several months. She wrote him a lot and prayed for him and asked me to pray for him as well. I did as she asked, even though I had a little nudge in me that was still unforgiving. I wasn't sure how to pray for him, because I really did not want to at that time. But because Hannah kept asking me to pray for her daddy, I did. As I began to pray, I heard the Lord say, "The more you pray for him, the more free you will become." I thought I had truly forgiven, because I had convinced myself that I had forgiven him. I confessed I had forgiven him, but when someone would bring up his name or I would begin praying for him, I would have this "ugh" gut feeling, and judgmental thoughts would go through my mind. The Lord brought this scripture to my attention one day when I was reading my bible:

But I say unto you, love your enemies, bless them that curse you, do good to them that hate you, and pray for them which despitefully use you, and persecute you. **Matthew 5:44 KJV**

I immediately heard, "But I say unto you…" meaning He was talking to me! I remember saying, "Lord, do you realize what you are asking me to do?" Then I remembered Jesus hanging on the cross, asking God to forgive us, and saying, "for they know not what they do". I began to cry as I prayed. At first the prayers were out of obligation, because my daughter asked me to pray. Yet, the more I prayed for him, the lighter and easier it became. The bitterness began to leave, and it started becoming more heart felt. Then I developed a compassion deep within to see him truly set free and happy. Now, we no longer have any hard or bitter feelings towards each other, and I continue to pray for him even today.

Chapter 4

A Nightmare Reality

Around age 16, Hannah started dating a very sweet well-mannered young man, named Cameron. He drove a beautiful blue car. She thought he was so cool and talked about him all the time. Over the course of their relationship, he became like family to us. She acted like she was head over heels in love, but really had no understanding of what love was. Later, they started having trouble in their relationship and she told me he had been engaging in drugs. She said had caught him snorting something in the bathroom and they got into a major argument, which ended their relationship. She was devastated. Years later, she admitted to me that the first time she tried drugs was with Cameron. This is where it all began.

Not aware of the drug use before, there were really no signs that I could detect. Her attitude grew worse, but I thought it was just the teenage years and hormones. I thought nothing at all about drugs. Drugs just weren't her style, or so I thought. As time passed, she began to show more outburst of behavioral problems and started rebelling. At 18 years old, she intentionally started an argument with my husband, Trey, who was asleep on the couch. She'd gotten mad at my son, Bryson, for not letting her use his cell phone while she was grounded from her cell phone. During this heated argument, Bryson called me at work and told me what transpired. He told me that she threatened him that if he didn't let her use his phone, she was going to go start a big fuss with Trey on purpose. She had so much bitterness and hurt in her that she took it out on everyone around her to get what she wanted. While on the phone with Bryson, I could hear her in the background screaming, so I called my sister. I asked her to go get Hannah and keep her while I was at work, and she did. This was the day she moved out of our house and began to live with my sister. She met a guy, named Chris through her cousins, and dated him several years. They eventually moved in together, and in 2013 she became pregnant, giving birth to my precious granddaughter, Makayla in 2014. It seemed like their life was on track and they were doing so well and so happy.

One day I received a phone call from Hannah, and she was screaming and crying, saying that her and Chris were arguing. His mom and sister were there and were making her leave, so she needed a ride. I went to get her and the baby, but they had Makayla in the car and wouldn't let Hannah have her. With all the screaming and hysterical drama that Hannah was exhibiting, they began to tell me that she was abusing pain pills and mistreating Chris. They stated she was going to have to leave, because the home they lived in belonged to Chris' stepdad, Arnold. Finally, after all of Hannah's screaming and crying, she stated she wasn't leaving without her baby. Makayla was in the back seat of their car crying the whole time. To diffuse the situation, they decided it would be best to surrender Makayla to Hannah and me. I ensured them that Makayla would be well taken care of, I would make sure of that. Hannah denied the pill abuse to me when I talked to her on our way home. She placed the blame on them, stating they didn't like her and wanted to control everything. She was distraught. Shortly after this took place, we had a court hearing concerning the custody of Makayla. Hannah and Chris were given joint custody. Hannah had her for one week then Chris had her for one week.

Things seemed to be going well. Hannah got a great job, and a nice car to drive. Makayla loved their car, she called it, "mine and mommy's car." Hannah began to occasionally go hang out with a friend she knew from work, and I would keep Makayla for a couple of hours if it happened to be Hannah's custody week. Then, Hannah began to stay gone a lot on the weeks that she didn't have Makayla. She would spend the night with her "friend". I eventually got to meet her friend, Paul, and he was a very well-mannered, well dressed guy. I never would have imagined that Paul used any type of drugs. I didn't picture addicts looking so nicely kept. I didn't think they'd be so calm and polite. He definitely played his cards right around me.

One week when we didn't have Makayla, Hannah called me at work and said she was going to spend the night with a friend and wouldn't be home that night. I was glad she had met some friends to hang out with and enjoy time with when Makayla was at her daddy's. I thought it would help her come out of the depressed state that she had been in since she had lost, what she called, "her perfect little family." To see her engaging in friendships and happy smiles again, made me happy. It wasn't until I was at work one day, about 45 minutes before my shift ended, when I received a bizarre phone call from Hannah, she was hysterical and saying, "HURRY! Momma come get me! They're going to kill me! Please hurry!" then she started screaming, "OH NO! They trying to break in the door!" She was beside herself! Needless to say, I was terrified! I said, "Who is trying to get you? Where are you at!?" Then she whispered, "Shhhh….They will hear you! Be quiet, they are coming!"

This went on a few more minutes, then, she hung up the phone! She was at such high levels of extreme fear and anxiety, I honestly thought someone was after her! I was a nervous wreck, trying to get her to tell me where she was and find out who was trying to get her! I started praying and panicking at the same time! "Lord, where is she!? Who is trying to get her?! And why?!" The phone number that showed up on my phone was a landline, so I called it back, and a lady answered, "Space convenient store." I told her that my daughter called me from that number hysterically upset saying someone was after her, trying to get in and kill her. I asked the lady if she had seen her and she replied, "Yes ma'am, she is here. I let her use the phone. She came running in the store asked to use the phone because someone was after her, trying to kill her. She was crying and shaking like a leaf, so I let her use the phone."

I asked the lady if she has seen anyone behind her, or if anything seemed suspicious? She stated, "No ma'am, I haven't seen anyone, but she says there is, and maybe they didn't want to come in the store when she came in. But I haven't even seen any cars go by other than hers. Her car is sitting in the parking lot, and I don't see anyone in the car with her." I asked her where Hannah was, and she stated she had locked herself in the bathroom, hiding. I asked the lady where this store was located, and she gave me the address. I immediately left work and headed to that store, but from where I work, it was about 40 mins to that store, so I called Mark's girlfriend, Julie, and asked if her and Mark would go check this out and I would meet them there, because I had no idea what was going on. I didn't know who or what I would encounter. As I was driving down the road, I received another call from Hannah from the same number! She was screaming and crying hysterical saying, "Hurry momma they're going to kill me! Please! Here they come! Hurry!" and the phone hung up again! I called the number back and got no answer this time. I really began to sweat. I started speeding down the road while praying and crying! I called Julie, and she said, "I'm almost there and you be careful." When I arrived, Julie and Hannah were in the parking lot talking to a policeman. Hannah was going on and on about what she perceived to be more real than the ones standing in front of her. When the policeman told me to step to the side and speak to him, he began to tell me that she was high on meth (short for methamphetamines), and I felt like I was going to faint! NOT MY DAUGHTER!! I wasn't sure how to deal with this, talk about TOTAL SHOCK!! I was feeling all kind of emotions from extreme anger to hurt to disappointment, like I had just been gutted! I was so mad that I felt like I was the one she better be afraid of and she better be glad that police were present when I found out! Next, I felt pure NUMBNESS! I felt almost paralyzed emotionally! I can't even explain how I truly felt, but I can say it was the WORST feeling I have ever experienced in my life. I asked the policeman, "So you mean there is no one really after her?" He stated, "No, she is hallucinating. She is fine, she just needs to go home until it wears off." I said, "You need to take her to jail until it wears off. If it was alcohol, you would. She is in no shape to drive like this. It's obvious she is under the influence of something much worse than alcohol!" He stated he couldn't take her in because she didn't have anything on her, no drugs or paraphernalia was found in her car or on her when he searched. I said, "Well, NO, she doesn't because it's in her body now!" He stated he had no grounds to arrest her, so she got in her car and drove to my house.

At home she told me that her friend had bought her lunch and must have put something in her drink because as soon as she drank it, she fell asleep. But, when she woke up, she thought someone was after her. She said she had never taken any kind of drug like that before, and that the police must have thought she was on something. Then she asked a good question. "How could he say what I was on if he didn't find anything? I didn't tell him anything to make him say that." She laid in her bed, but she stayed awake all night. Once she got home, she was quiet, because I went to bed, and I laid in bed and began to pray. I thought this was something that probably scared her so bad, surely, she would never touch any drug again! LITTLE DID I KNOW... THIS WAS JUST THE BEGINNING!

As time went by, she began to distance herself more from home, unless it was the week that she had Makayla. Those weeks she would come home from work, spend time with Makayla until bedtime, then ask me if she could go to Paul's house since Makayla would be going to bed. I began to notice her appearance starting to change. She began to lose weight, and her face would show more acne and bumps. At first, being so naïve or in plain denial, (I'm not quite sure which one.) I thought it was just her nerves from all the emotional trauma she had experienced recently. I also thought it could be the worry of the new job, being a single mother, or starting her life over. I just wouldn't accept the fact that she had indeed, truly turned to drugs, much less to this extreme. How could I, being her momma and being so close for the most part, NOT SEE THIS COMING?

After a while, Hannah began making new "friends". I began to meet more and more people as she would call me and mention another "new name" or bring them to the house when changing clothes or getting something. I started to see just where things were going based on the looks of some of them and the distinctive smell on each one of their clothes. I can detect that smell anywhere! It has forever burned a scent in my nostrils for sure! Then I saw a post that brought a very deep sadness to my heart as I was scrolling through Facebook. I saw a picture of Hannah that to this day gives me chills to look at! From the most gorgeous radiant smile in the past, I saw a picture of Hannah standing with her head hanging down, her long hair hanging down to one side of her face and over one eye. Her eyes looking down as if shame and total discouragement had taken complete hold of her with no hope of return. The smile was gone... the saddest look on her face, but it wasn't just a look that portrayed sadness. When I saw it, it's like I saw darkness and .... LIKE A COMPLETE EMPTINESS! It was as if darkness had taken the glow from her. It wasn't just a covering, it was GONE!!! I began to cry from the deepest part within me! It was as if I felt what she felt, and that is when it became a reality to me that this was not just a one-time incident. Now, it was going to be a major fight in the spirit realm for my daughter's life.

Chapter 5

Consider the Cost

As I tried to process this nightmare that had now become a reality in our lives, it seemed to get worse as fear started to flood me. I didn't know where to begin trying to process it all. I was completely consumed with the feeling of hopelessness. I never felt more alone in my life, thinking, surely no one else could ever feel the deep gutting feeling that I felt at that point. It was as if she were a complete stranger, like I didn't know her at all. We weren't able to speak to each other without her getting extremely angry at me. If I tried to talk to her about what she was doing, she denied that she was on any drugs. But it was definitely obvious she was doing something that altered her way of thinking and acting. Eventually she lost her job, therefore giving her a lot of extra free time to spend with these people she claimed to be her friends. She would allow random "friends" to drive her car, and occasionally would call me and tell me to come pick her up. "Pick you up? Where is your car?" She would say that "they" had her car, and she couldn't get hold of "them" on the phone. I would tell her that she needed to get her car and drive it, that she was not leaving her car with "them." Soon after, she called and said that she had her car and she was fine but didn't return home that evening.

When I would try to reason with her, she would become irate and start hollering at me and cursing. That had never been her personality towards me before all this started. It was as if she had no conscience at all. One day she came home and said she was taking Makayla with her to a friend's house. I knew she was high, because she acted very sketchy and nervous like. I told her she wasn't taking Makayla with her to anyone's house I didn't know. She grabbed Makayla and said, "She's my baby and I will take her where I want to! Do you think I'm stupid, I would never take her anywhere that she could get hurt! I know what I'm doing!"

I argued with her because I knew she really wasn't capable of making good and rational decisions. She wasn't making the best choices for herself much less for Makayla. She started buckling Makayla into her car seat while I tried to reason with her to leave Makayla with me. She refused. When she got into the driver's seat, I tried to go around the car to the side Makayla was on, and she backed up and put the car in drive and came straight towards me trying to run over me! I jumped back and slapped the side of the car, and she immediately stopped the car as if it stunned her, Makayla was crying by then and she screamed at me, "You're scaring her! Ok! get her out this time, but I promise you, you will regret it!" I went around to Makayla's door and got her out and told Hannah to leave. She spun off out of the driveway. She would come and go often, bring people with her that she would call her friends. They always seemed to be very well behaved and respectful, although I could clearly see they were as high as Hannah was. I was nice to them, although I didn't trust them. My husband on the other hand, was very intolerant of them. He knew the drug world well. Fourteen years prior, he was making his own batch of methamphetamines along with doing other drugs. During that time, he ran with some of these same people and their families, with whom my daughter was now affiliated with. After going to prison, losing his first wife and two children, his home, job, integrity, self-esteem, and even the desire to live due to all this, he had a zero-tolerance policy. He didn't want them anywhere near our home. He said he didn't want her bringing anyone to that house, if something gets stolen, he knew who was at fault. He tried to tell her what all she was in for in this game, and she made out like we were crazy. She said they weren't on drugs. We were just trying to run her life. After talking to her and trying to get her to understand why we felt this way, we offered to help her get help or go to rehab. She really blew up! She got in her car and left.

As time went on, the behaviors became more monstrous. During another custody week, Hannah tried to take Makayla with her again to someone's house. I knew this person was an active drug addict. I wouldn't let Hannah take her, and she started hollering and grabbed Makayla up and went flying through the house as if she was going to leave. I stood in front of the door, and Hannah lifted her arm as if she was going to hit me. Makayla was crying, and Hannah ran into my bedroom with her. As I raced behind her so she didn't lock the door where I couldn't get in, she tried to open the window because I shut the door in behind me and wouldn't let her out with the baby.

Crystal Owens

Makayla at the time was 2 years old. I had my phone in my pocket, and I called 911. She frantically tried to get out of the windows, and I stood in front of the windows. When she tried the door, I stood in front of the door. She was screaming in the phone while I was talking to the 911 operator, saying, "She's holding me hostage! Help! She won't let me out of this room!" The operator said, "Ma'am, I have an officer on the way."

When I told Hannah that the police were on the way, she handed Makayla to me and said, "Here, now let me out of here!" (with a few curse words) As soon as I opened the bedroom door, Hannah took off running, jumped in her car, while shooting me birdies and hollering curse words out the window as she drove off spinning wheels out of my driveway. This was the day I had to make the hardest decision of my life! I had to look out for the best interest of my sweet granddaughter. I knew I had no rights as a grandparent to protect her from her mother who loved her so much. Yet, the drugs had Hannah so bound that she wanted to expose Makayla to places and people she didn't need to be exposed to. With Hannah being Makayla's mother and me having no legal papers to keep her from taking her from me, Hannah could legally come and get Makayla anytime against my will. So, as she got more persistent about wanting to take Makayla with her, things began to heat up between Hannah and me. I was so upset thinking she could come and get this baby and there is nothing I could do about it, so in desperation, I called Makayla's other grandmother, Chris's mother. I asked her if we could work together to make sure Makayla was safe. I asked her if she would talk with Chris and

43

see if something could be done. That was the hardest decision I think I've ever made, not knowing what would lie ahead, yet I felt I had the responsibility to protect Makayla even at the expense of seeing my own grandchild. As time progressed and court hearings took place, Hannah eventually lost joint custody of Makayla, and Chris was awarded full custody of Makayla. As we walked out of the court room into the hallway, Hannah said to me, "Well I hope you know, you just put a bullet in my head!" and walked out the door. It really became a battle at that point, because Hannah really got heavier into the drug game with no responsibilities. She began to stay in dangerous places with multiple drug users and dealers.

Very early one morning, my husband received a phone call from Hannah. She was crying and saying, "Come get me! They are mad and fighting. The police are on the way, and they won't give me my keys to leave in my car!" My husband asked where she was at. She stated she was at Super 8 motel with a bunch of others, and she was scared to death. She'd seen a girl, named Angie, shoot up and miss the vein. Blood went shooting out of her arm, and Hannah started screaming because this was the first time she had ever seen this and it traumatized her. My husband and I left and went to the motel to pick her up and she was shaking and crying. I took my husband home and took my daughter to the hospital due to her mental state. She requested to go, but by the time the doctor came in, she jumped up and said, "Let's go!" I tried to talk her into seeing a doctor for her anxiety and she said, "I'm fine, I don't need to see a doctor," so we left.

Angie had gotten arrested that night along with a couple of other people at the motel. Angie had Hannah's car keys locked in her car, so Hannah couldn't get her keys because Angie's car was locked while she was in jail. The next day, Hannah and another friend, Angie's daughter, go get the keys out of Angie's car, while a police officer watched Hannah remove her items from the vehicle. However, when Angie got out of jail, she said items were stolen, and took a warrant out on Hannah for this. She started on the path of making herself a court record. Not long after this incident, she had several unpleasant incidents with Angie. She would call me briefly almost every day, even though a lot of times it would end up in arguments because she would call me for money which I started saying, "NO!" But despite the arguments, she always called me to tell me where she was, and who she was with, even if I wasn't going be pleased with it. One evening she came to the house with a girl I had never met before. They were taking pictures of themselves in the yard, and laughing, but I knew they were high. They kept their sunglasses on to try and cover it up, but I knew. The very next morning, she called me from a cellphone number I didn't recognize. She sounded very groggy as she told me Angie and the girl she had with her at the house just the day before, had drugged her drink and choked her out with a crowbar. By this time, I was skeptical to listen to all this non-sense, or so I thought it was, but she had asked me to come to Gardo's motel because she was in the parking lot and hurting. I asked her where her car was, and she stated she didn't know for sure but she guessed they had it. I went to pick her up and she used my phone to call one of the guys that was with them. He met her friend to get the car and keys and later that evening, we met her to give it back. I tried to get her to go to get help and go to rehab, but she refused over and over, insisting she was fine, that there was nothing wrong with her.

I didn't know what to do as it seemed she was getting deeper and deeper into drug addiction. My beautiful, sweet daughter had become someone I didn't even know! I prayed and prayed a lot! But at times it was as if I didn't know what to pray, how to pray, and even have the strength to pray anymore! I knew there was no other way she was coming out of this without prayer. Sometimes I would just start to pray and felt like I had no idea what words to speak because of the agonizing pain deep down in my soul. At that point I would just begin to pray in the spirit and such an uncontrollable cry would rush out so heavy that I would curl up into a fetal position and ask God to HELP ME! I DON'T KNOW HOW TO PRAY LORD! I CAN'T DO THIS LORD! PLEASE HELP ME! Honestly the yearning pains were so heavy and deep at times, that it was as if I was in actual labor. This stronghold of drug addiction seemed as though it was fully anchored and keeping her in place. I felt completely helpless! There were so many encounters with bad reports. It seemed like day after day after day, I received phone calls from Hannah, wanting money. I would tell her no, she would get very irritated cursing and saying horrible comments just to hurt me. Through it all, God began to show me how to deal with this type of rebellious behavior.

It was a beautiful weekend on October 30, 2016. I was getting so tired of all the craziness that was going on around me, and my husband said, "I know you have been wanting to see the leaves changing colors at Blue Ridge Mountain Parkway, so we are going to go riding. We need to get away from here anyway." So, we packed up and went to meet a friend, his girlfriend, and his dad and we went riding all day. It was gorgeous, the most colorful leaves and view I have ever seen! As we were coming home, our friends went another way towards their town, and Trey and I went in the direction of our home. As we got about 20 mins from our house, we passed this huge mountain that caught my eye. As if it was a magnet, I stared at it until it was completely out of sight, because as I was looking at it I heard the Lord begin speaking to me. He said, "Don't you be afraid, and don't you run! This mountain is not greater than I AM!" All of a sudden, something rose up in me, and I was squinting my eyes and talking to that mountain. I said, "You are not greater than God! This mountain of rebellion and addiction, you will NOT take my daughter out! I am NOT afraid of you and I will not bow to how you show yourself to me. Sin is only good for a season! And your season is almost up!" I began to hear loudly the scripture:

Greater is he that is in you, than he that is in the world. **1 John 4:4 (KJV)**

So, I started saying to that mountain, "Greater is he that is in ME, than he that is in the world! I will not be afraid of what man can do to me! No weapon formed against me shall prosper in the name of Jesus!" After this encounter I felt like I had a boldness so strong that nothing could bring me down. At the time, I did not realize this was the word God was giving me ahead of time for strength to endure the events that would occur later in this journey.

Chapter 6

What You Focus on Determines Your Outcome

Thanksgiving of 2016 rolled around, being at work helped with not focusing on the chaos around me. But, when Christmas of 2016 rolled around, I could have, and almost did succumb to the circumstances; as depression, hopelessness, discouragement, despair, grief, and all the bad feelings that tried to creep in and ruin the holiday. I wasn't sure if we would even see Hannah that year for Christmas, or if we would be allowed to see our sweet granddaughter even though we had gifts for her. I remember walking through the living room, going to the kitchen, when I saw my husband sitting at the table wrapping Makayla's gifts, and tears just rolling down his face. He wasn't saying a word. He didn't have to; I knew exactly why he was crying, and I knew how he felt. I too, began to cry as I walked over to him and hugged him from the back and told him, "I don't know how, but God will restore our family just like He intended for it to be. Just pray and believe God is hearing our prayers and He will answer. I know in my heart we will get to see Makayla and give her our gifts ourselves." He just nodded his head, "yes" and kept wrapping.

When I returned to my bedroom to wrap the presents I'd purchased for Trey and a few family members, I remember saying out loud to myself, "This too shall pass, I will be like the psalmist David, I will encourage myself in the Lord!" *(1 Samuel 30:6)*

So, I refused to pity my situation. As I fought my feelings of defeat, I put my earbuds in and began to listen to songs with prayers by Clint Brown. I listened to some Christmas songs off the Avalion Christmas Album, "We Are the Reason" and I began to feel a heat sensation coming over me. I started to sing that song to the Lord, and while singing the lyrics, I changed the wording to "she" saying, "SHE is the reason that you gave your life, SHE is the reason that you suffered and died, in a world that was lost you gave all you could give, to give HER a reason to live!" If you've never heard this song, I HIGHLY recommend it. This song really touches my heart every time I hear it, I tend to listen to it even throughout the year not just Christmas, because he truly did all he did for every human being. He truly loves each and every person that has ever been and ever will be created. His love is not on the condition of who you are, how well you are known, the amount of money you make or how poor you are, whether you are saved or a sinner, whether you are living a good clean life or whether you are a drug addict or even the dealer himself. Jesus did it all for ALL! The same opportunity stands for every person and all I could see when I listened to that song repeatedly that day was, seeing all those bound in drugs, their families and their children, and I cried as I was seeing Jesus saying I did this for you.

Next, I began to sing the song, "Happy Birthday Jesus, I'm so glad it's Christmas… etc., but the real gift is you!" I CHOSE to focus on Jesus. I made a conscience decision to praise Him! He is the REAL reason for the season, and my heart was breaking as I broke out into praying for these people, most of them I didn't even know. Some of them I didn't care to know, but Jesus was letting me see how He sees them, and my heart began to break and cry out for them! Suddenly, an awesome feeling came over me that was the purest love I have EVER experienced. I was deep into worship and all that was on my heart was those who were bound in drug addictions and the children who were losing their mothers, fathers, and families. I was crying so hard, but also had such an awesome peace I cannot explain. I had to just bring the whole box of Kleenex to where I was wrapping presents! The presence (not presents) of God became so heavy that I fell into interceding for these people. I heard the Lord say:

Love one another, as I have loved you.

*Greater love hath no man than this, that a man lay down his life for his friends. (**John 15: 12-13**) KJV*

I asked the Lord, "How to lay do I lay my life down for another?" I knew He wasn't talking about me literally dying for them, even though this scripture is referring to Jesus laying his life down for us in death. I heard him say, "love them and pray for them." I started visualizing the families made whole again and enjoying holidays together in love, peace, and joy. The visions was so intense that it seemed real to me. It felt much realer than the gloom and despair that was lurking around me. I just completely refused to allow the circumstances dictate my day and steal my joy.

Later that day, I was in the kitchen, fixing some food for our other three grown children when Hannah came in. I wasn't sure if I would see her or not, being the state of mind she was in, but there she was. She came in walking fast and talking fast and said, "Hey momma, Merry Christmas! I have to hurry, I have someone in my car waiting on me." I told her that Trey and I had discussed what to give her for Christmas, as we usually give the children money, per their request. However, due to the circumstances we only gave her $40. She was fine with that.

She didn't argue, she just took the money and said, "Thank you momma. I love you. It will be better next year, I promise."

I choked up for a minute and said, "Yes ma'am, it sure will be. God promised me my children! I love you and most of all Jesus loves you!"

She smiled and said, "I know He does," as she left. Although it was only a brief moment and all the children and granddaughter weren't there at the same time, I was still beyond grateful to the Lord for allowing me to see her at all that day. Later that afternoon we were able to see our granddaughter Makayla to give her presents from Maw Maw and Paw Paw. Then the other three children came over to see us. As much as I could have complained and rolled in the pity, I chose to focus on what I

Crystal Owens

had been blessed with that day, God's love and blessings, for which I was very thankful.

I said aloud, "Thank you Lord, your mercies are new every morning! Your grace is sufficient in my weakness!" I thought to myself, at least she is alive so I was able to hug her even for a moment, unlike some less fortunate families who were sitting with family while missing someone who was tragically lost this year. I truly believe the Lord blessed me that day because I kept my focus on Him. I quickly recognized this was the Lord's doing, and I was beyond grateful . This was a life changing experience for sure. It truly began to change the way I perceived others through the eyes of God. It was almost as if this was the way Jesus was seeing each one of us, while on the cross praying, "Father, forgive them, for they know not what they do," as he focused on us while looking down through the scope of time.

53

Chapter 7

Comfort or Correct

I had dealt with Hannah many times about getting help with her addiction. I'd tried to encourage her to go to rehab but she constantly refused and denied the fact that she even did drugs. She would get mad at me and say that I was her momma and should just let her come home. I told her to get a job and work towards getting her life in order and I would help her. But I refused to enable her habitual lifestyle knowing she had no real intentions of change. Over and over we went through the same arguments as if she didn't even see she had a problem. She always acting like everyone else was the one with a problem and it was everyone else's fault for what she was doing, because no one would help her. However, until she was ready for help, no matter what we did it wasn't good enough and it wasn't going to make her change her ways. I prayed every day for her.

One night, towards the end of December 2016, I had just laid down in the bed, was watching tv, and Hannah called. She said, "Momma, I'm hungry and I'm freezing!" (now I need to say she was in her car that had heat). I had already been trying to reason with her earlier that day on the phone about getting help, and she cursed me for not giving her money.

I said, "Hannah, I don't know what to tell you. I've tried to help you and you refuse to get help!"

She replied, "It's 29 degrees out here and I'm freezing!" She called me a few choice words, and said, "You can't even fix me a (blank) sandwich, some (blank) momma you are! You can't even help me ..."

I knew it had to be the Lord, because I just calmly said, "Hannah, I'm your momma. I'm not your savior. Right now, you need a savior, and I am not Him! Go call on the Lord." Then I hung up the phone, and burst out crying. I said, "Lord, do I not even love my own child? What is wrong with me!?" I heard the Lord say, "As long as you are her comfort zone, I never will be." At that point I threw my hands up in the air and said, "I can't do this Lord, I give her to you completely. If you can't help her Lord, and you being God, I know I can't!" I heard Him quietly say, "I can be where she is. I can be in places that you can't be to protect her. But I can't if you don't give her to me. Hannah needs her Father," He said.

I said, "What do you mean?"

"A Father provides, protects, and corrects, and she needs it all. A mother loves and nurtures. There is a time for each role, and in this she would die with only the mother's care, she needs her Father."

I said, "I know Lord, but I can't do anything about that."

"I am her Father. Let me do what only I can do."

So, at that point, I gave her to the Lord and laid down in the bed. As I was watching tv, all of a sudden I heard, "You just going to let her starve and freeze to death, while you laying here in this warm king size bed, watching that big tv, and you can just walk right into the kitchen and eat whatever you want, while you let your own child starve and freeze, what a momma you are!" I knew this was the enemy, so I jumped up out of bed, and I grabbed my bible, and held it up in the air, and I said, out loud, "Lord this is your word! YOU promised me my children, and I don't know how you're going to take care of this, but I refuse to fear. I know you are WELL ABLE." By doing that out loud, it shut out that voice trying to bring guilt and condemnation, when I sat down on the bed I opened my bible and it almost immediately went to this scripture, which I had never read before, but I know it was the Lord who lead me to it, at that very moment, that I needed a word of confirmation from Him.

> But thus saith the Lord, Even the captives of the mighty shall be taken away, and the prey of the terrible shall be delivered: for I will contend with him that contendeth with thee, and I will save thy children. *Isaiah 49:25 (KJV)*

OH MY! How that word just grabbed my heart, it just LEAPED IN MY SPIRIT! And those last few words let me KNOW, it was for God to do, not me! When he said, "I will contend with him... and I will save your children!" It was all the faith I needed to completely let her go into God's care. I

knew that no matter what the enemy or even my own conscience said, I knew I was free from the condemnation and guilt
and even the pressure at that moment! I jumped up out of the
bed again, and said, "Here ya go devil! God said HE WOULD
TAKE CARE OF YOU because people are not my problem,
you are! **GOD SAID HE WOULD SAVE MY CHIL-
DREN!** I can't save her, but He can and He will. YOU
MIGHT TOUCH HER BUT YOU CAN'T TAKE HER
OUT because I'm holding God to His word which is forever
settled in heaven!"

From that day forward, it was as if that word in Isaiah 49:25 is
branded in my heart! I wrote it down on an index card, and I
took it with me everywhere I went. If I started feeling afraid
that something wasn't right or heard bad news from her or
about her I would immediately take that index card out, hold it
up, and say "Lord, this your word! You gave me this word yourself. I didn't even know it was in the bible, but you gave it to
me. I know you are able to deliver and save my daughter! I bring
this scripture to your remembrance and I hold you to this word.
Thank you that you have her in your care and you protect her!"
Shortly, peace would come over me and I could go on about
my day without being afraid or worried. Still to this day, I use
this scripture for her and even our other children. My mother
knew how much I clung to that scripture and how important it
is to me. She made a double glass frame, one side has our children and the other side has a decorated picture with this scripture in it. It sits right under my tv in my bedroom, the tv I watch
the most. I see it every day, multiple times, and I remember

each time, that I can't save my children, but God promises me
HE WILL!

Chapter 8

Insane Behaviors

Despite the Lord's promises, the enemy kept trying to stop me. In January of 2017, Hannah had come by the house with another new face, a guy that was obviously as high as a kite! He was driving her vehicle, and I asked her, "Who is that?" She told me his name and said the same routine, "He's a good person, and he's clean. He doesn't do drugs!" Well to hear her tell it, NONE OF THEM DID! So, the next day she called me and gave me his phone number and told me to call him. She said he left in her car without her permission while she was in the shower. I called and got no answer. I got mad and called back and left a not so nice message and told him if he didn't call back or bring that car back, I would call and report it missing, because it was on my insurance. I received no response from him, and neither did she. I was so frustrated with these types of people, including my own child, that I was ready to just deal with them all myself! It was so frustrating to deal with, that when I prayed, I would say things like, "Lord, get those people off the streets that are into the drug dealing and deal with them!" It wasn't really much of a heart prayer. I was more or less telling Him how to deal with them and what was wrong with them, as if I knew and as if my daughter was better than them. Then the Lord began to deal with me on a personal level. He told me, "I want you to start writing the names down of all those she is affiliated with and start praying for them. A lot of these people don't have people and families who pray for them like Hannah does."

I replied, "Lord, do you know what you are asking me to do?"

He said, "I love them as much as I love your daughter!"

I never thought of that. I knew He did, but hearing Him tell me, pricked my heart! So, I made a list of every person I'd met, heard of through her, or even pictures or tags from Facebook with her. Once the list was compiled, I started praying for them. Soon, I noticed the more I prayed for them, the more compassion I began to feel towards them. The Lord reminded me of this scripture in Ephesians:

> *For we wrestle not against flesh and blood, but against principalities, against powers, against the rulers of the darkness of this world, against spiritual wickedness in high places.* **Ephesians 6:12 (KJV)**

He reminded me that it wasn't people that was my problem, it was the enemy, and that these people were just as bound as Hannah.

A few days later, I received a phone call from a detective that asked me if I had any idea how to get hold of Hannah? I told him yes and gave him her phone number. He proceeded to tell me that her car had been totaled by an individual she had been hanging around with for some time. A policeman was going to do a routine stop, when the person driving the vehicle refused to stop. This person took them on a high-speed chase and eventually rolled the vehicle. Afterwards, he jumped out and ran through the woods before he was eventually caught and taken to jail. The police also informed me that they found a bag of methamphetamine on the ground on the same trail they chased the guy on. The detective questioned me about the vehicle, asked if I knew who the guy would have been. I told him who had come by my house with Hannah the day before the car was taken out of her possession, and what she had told me earlier that week. He asked me if she had reported that vehicle stolen? I told him that I tried to get her to, but the last time I had asked her about it she said he would bring it back. She had spoken to his cousin about it, but as a result of her just letting it go for some time, she lost her car because they said it was totaled. At that point, she was back and forth from this house to that house and caught rides with others that she was hanging around. I would occasionally talk to her. She would call me and come by. It seemed like she was always with someone I had never met, so I got to meet a lot of new people. I wasn't very happy with the situations, but as I said earlier, they were very nice to me and I couldn't change her or even them.

Hannah called me a few days later and told me that a well-known TV preacher that she watched a lot on tv was going to be calling me, I was like, "OK…" totally not believing her at all. I knew their schedules were busy. She said she got ahold of him through social media, which I didn't believe either. They would rarely ever even respond to social media much less contact you through it. Less than an hour had went by and I received a phone call from a number that wasn't familiar. I answered and he stated his name, as the name of this particular TV preacher. He stated that he just spoke with Hannah and that she had contacted him wanting to be free of her addictions. As he talked, I listened closely to see if it was indeed this particular one, because I could recognize the voice, and it was indeed this preacher. He told me she had contacted him through social media and he normally doesn't respond to social media but that the Lord told him to respond to her. She'd said she wanted to be delivered and be free of drugs. She had told him that she listened to him every day and he was the preacher who changed her life. So he asked me if I could bring her to see him and I told him yes. I told him I had been praying for her and knew it was from the Lord because I asked God to send someone her way that she would listen to, but I never knew it would be that extreme. God knows exactly who we will hear, who we have respect for, and who we will listen to. In Hannah's case it was this particular well-known TV preacher, who has thousands of people who probably bombard him daily, but God singled her out just for this one situation. God knew she believed in that avenue, and He honored it. It goes to show just how far God will go when we get serious with Him!

I've learned that we have to take the impossibilities off of God, let God be God, just ask Him and believe He is able, and let him do the work. Now there was nothing magical in the preacher because of who he is or the fact he is well known or even on TV. It was HER faith that even caused God to be able to use that route. And yes! She was still on drugs, and still high as a kite, but she could STILL reach God when she cried out for help, truly wanting a change. He heard her, and moved on her behalf. We went a couple of nights later to see him as he said, and he came up to me and hugged me and told me that God will bring her out and for me to just trust the Lord. I cried and thanked him for obeying the Lord when he said to respond. Then he went to Hannah and talked to her and brought her up to the front of the church with him. He told the congregation who she was and what she had said and that she wanted to be free. Then he commanded the enemy to loose her and prayed over her and she cried. He hugged her and it was as if her countenance had changed just in an instance. After service we left, and I took my mother home. Hannah and I started down the road and she started getting really agitated. It was as if the devil himself were in the car with me. She began fussing and when I wouldn't go where she wanted and do what she wanted, she started kicking the seat, and the car window. I stopped the car in the middle of the highway and told her to get out. She screamed and said, "I'm not getting out here." I drove to the place she was staying at. She started jerking and kicking the door after I opened it as if to knock it off the hinges. She said, "I can't go in there now. It's too late they won't let me in!" So, I drove down the road a little and told her she wasn't going with me anywhere acting like that because Trey would run her off. She screamed, "I don't want to go to your house anyway," then proceeded to kick my seat in the car. By then, my patience had worn very thin, and I honestly was ready to drag her out myself and beat her butt. However, I also knew there was a spiritual battle going on within her and she didn't even know how to deal with it herself. I felt bad for her, yet I wanted to FIX her myself!

Finally, I got to the store and she said, "Stop at this store and buy me some cigarettes!"

I said, "I don't smoke and I'm not buying you any cigarettes."

She said, "Well, I'm thirsty can you AT LEAST buy me a drink?"

So, I stopped at the store and gave her few dollars to go into store, and she said, "I'm not going in, you go in and get it!"

I thought to myself, so you can hotwire my car and steal it and leave me here? I told her, "NO! I gave you the money and if you want it, you can go inside and get what you are wanting."

Again, she started raising her voice and hollering and cussing, and few minutes later a policeman pulled up (not because of us) and went in store. When he came back out, I told him to make her get out of my car, and I explained the situation. He made her get out of the car, and I drove off. As I drove, I started crying and told the Lord, "Lord, I don't know what to do anymore! But I trust you. I know you will take care of her."

By the time I got home, a friend of hers texted me that Hannah walked across the road where the friend was working and for me to not worry. She had taken Hannah to her house. Her friend told me she was so sorry for what I was going through as her mom! I knew God would take care of her and I was thankful He let me know she was ok and that he had it all worked out. Just a few days following this, I actually did notice that she was doing much better with her attitude.

There were so many instances that tried to discourage me from God's promise. Here are a few in short detail; the first of February, Hannah had come to the house with another new friend, or a new person to me. They were outside posing and taking pictures and asked if I would take pictures of them in front of the cross that is in the yard (on the cover of this book). Then they left. The next day around 8am, Hannah called me and said, "come to Gardo's motel and pick me up." At first, I said no, and she proceeded to tell me that "they" had put something in her drink and that Angie and another girl had choked her out with a crowbar, and said as she was passing out, "REST IN PEACE!" (RIP) She then stated that she woke up in the parking lot of this motel.

There was a time that she was going to get help at the hospital, and they sent in a mental health specialist, who evaluated her mental stability. They asked her some serious questions and she was answering them. At the end, they decided she needed treatment for her depression and hopelessness. They were going to admit her, and she freaked out, and told me she was not staying. She got up and told me to come on because she wasn't staying in no crazy house. The lady then offered her outpatient help which she agreed to, but once we left the hospital, she told me that they were stupid. She said she didn't need them to help her. But I knew it was more than that. She didn't want help at the time, and she wasn't ready to give up the life she had been living. So, instead she would shift all faults and guilt elsewhere so she wouldn't have to accept the responsibilities for her own life.

Another night, it was freezing cold and she had no car at this time. She went to the hospital, and spent the night in the lobby, but refused to go to rehab or a shelter or anywhere that could possibly provide any kind of treatment. She slept in lobby that night and spent another night in an old abandoned building.

One evening she called me and was in the woods, stated she was running down the train tracks, because the police was watching the house she was staying at. One time she also said they came in on them and she run out of the house.

In March, my husband and I went to Florida for his back surgery, and we were going to be gone for a little over a week. My husband asked my son, Bryson, to stay at our house to watch over the house and tend to the animals. One night, Bryson called Trey and asked him if his dad was using our truck, Trey replied, I don't know he might be, but I wouldn't think he would be getting it this late, because it was around 9 o'clock pm. Trey told Bryson to call and ask him if he was using it. But instead, Bryson decided to follow the truck, while he called his pawpaw. His pawpaw said no he wasn't using the truck, so Bryson followed the truck to the little country store up the road. When it pulled up to the gas tanks, he blocked the truck in, and his sister, Hannah got out of the truck! Bryson, got out with his handgun, pointed it at her and told her to get that truck home, RIGHT NOW! He said, "I'm watching over the house while they are gone, and you are not stealing it while I'm here!" About that time, a guy got out of a vehicle beside where Bryson was standing and started towards him. Bryson turned the gun to him and told him he better get back or he would take care of him too. The guy hollered at Hannah and said, "COME ON! YOU ARE GOING TO GET US KILLED!" Bryson told her to take that truck home now and he was going to follow her. Then Bryson called the police and told them to come out to the house. Hannah drove the truck back to our house and she knew the police were on the way, so she pulled the truck in, jumped out and ran through the yard towards the pasture. She ran into the electric fence, then rolled under the fence to the barn. The police arrived and took a report from my son, and he was a nervous wreck. He even told on himself about pulling the gun out at the store. They didn't charge him or anything, they just told him if he had any more problems to call them back. So later, Hannah and I were talking, and she said, "That fence numbed me! Like I was paralyzed for a minute," and at that time we could laugh about it.

It seemed like every time I turned around, something dramatic was happening, she called me one evening and said that the guy that she was hanging around with had held her down, choked her, and almost broke her neck. She said she was in the woods hiding. I asked her where she was at. She said she didn't know, and then said that he called two girls to come over there and jump on her while he tried to hold her. She said she kicked one in the face and took off running. I don't really know how she got out of that situation, unless she called someone to come get her that knew where this particular guy lived. The only thing I know for sure is that God kept His promises to me to protect her.

I can remember so many things that happened, that really gave me every opportunity to worry, but it was as if God literally had me comforted in His great big hand of love! Now, that's the peace of God that passes all understanding! *(Philippians 4:7-KJV)*

Chapter 9

Mercy or Revenge

Early one morning in June, I woke up to get ready for work. I picked up my phone to check the time, as my husband and I rarely ever use an alarm clock. There were several missed calls and a message from a number I didn't recognize. I usually keep my phone on silent at night so I didn't hear anything, because Hannah would call from any number and at any hour, as they all rarely slept. Since I had put her in the Lord's hands a while back, I didn't worry. I trusted Him to take care of her. But as I checked the message, I was thrown by what I saw! It wasn't a text, but a picture of my daughter's face swollen and bruised! At the time, she had no phone minutes, and staying from house to house, all I could do was call this number back whom I received the message from. It was a girl that had been friends with Hannah most of her teenage years. They had their differences at times, since being in the drug situations, but for the most part, they were good friends. When she answered the phone, I asked, "Who is this?" she told me, and I asked her, "Who did this to Hannah?" and she told me who the girl was and what had happened. She told me where they all were when it happened. She said that she took Hannah with her when she got into the room because they shut the door when they saw her videoing. She said she couldn't help Hannah because she was 8 months pregnant. She tried to help Hannah after they left, then took Hannah to her house. I told her to have Hannah call me when she woke up, because she said Hannah took something for pain, and finally had fallen asleep. I was on my way to work, so I said just let her rest. Later, Hannah called me, and she said she felt like her face was broke and her whole body ached so bad. We both cried as I begged her to please go get help and get away from those people before something bad happened!

At first, I thought, I really didn't want to see the video, but it heated me more and more to know that there was one. I texted her and another girl that was there until they finally sent me the video. They hesitated for a day or so, which only made me angrier. Finally, I received the video. There wasn't just one girl, there were two girls! One was much larger in size than Hannah, the other was about her size. First of all, they didn't just jump her, they busted into the door and jumped her while she was in bed. She never even had a chance to defend herself! If it would have been a one on one fight and a fair fight, I wouldn't have been so upset! But after watching this with my very own eyes, I BECAME ENRAGED! It was like, something jumped inside of me and I had forgotten all that the Lord had taught me about love, forgiveness, and compassion! I don't know why, but I watched it over and over again, and to see the big girl hold her down while the other girl beat her in the face, repeatedly, caused a hatred in me that seemed like a fire with constant fueling flames! All I could hear roaring in my head was the big girl, screaming in her face…. "Kick me again, and I'll break your (blank-blank) kneecaps!!" She screamed many vulgar curse

70

words that only the devil himself would repeat, cursing her and calling her horrible names, let alone using God's name in vain every other breath! Then she proceeded to hold her and scream… "Let me tell you something, Little girl! Let me tell you! Little girl!"

OH MY! How this rang in my head and the vision of that video over and over just consumed my thinking to the point that I began to seek revenge myself. I was so far gone that I had it all planned out in my mind! It became so strong in me that I became afraid of myself! I would constantly hear and see this video replay over and over in my mind, while I was awake and in my sleep. I was consumed to say the least! I would think evil thoughts! I'd be alone and see and hear it and say out loud, "I want that big girl! She thinks she so BIG and BAD! Her mouth is as big as she is! She will think, she is a little girl!" I also thought about it taking two people to jump one person, "must not be as BAD as people think they are if it takes two to do the job! It is a wimp's way of doing things! I might not be the toughest person in the world, but when it comes to my child and this, *OH YEAH, I DON'T NEED TWO AND I DON'T NEED A DRUG TO GIVE ME THE ENERGY OR STRENGTH!! YOU JUST GAVE ME ALL THE IN-SENTIVE AND POWER I NEED! I'LL TAKE CARE OF THESE TWO MYSELF!* There isn't anybody bullet proof!"

I thought that I would do them exactly like they did her, catch them at their most vulnerable moment, unexpected, with no chance to guard themselves. I thought, "I'll let them look fear

71

right in the eye, with NO CHANCE TO ESCAPE!" And yes! I truly had this mindset, a fierce hatred and revenge within me. At the time, I felt like I was 10 feet tall and made of iron!!! I felt like a super-human figure. It was very real, and it was very scary! I was honestly afraid I wouldn't be able to control these feelings without carrying them through!

I could actually see it played out in my mind and I said, "OK, here's what I'm going do! I'm going to park my car at the church across the road from the well-known road for drug activity which the one girl lived on. I'm going to go hide in the ditch beside the road, and when they come down that road to the stop sign, I'm going to shoot them both! They won't have a chance to do it to anyone else!" Because, from what I had been told, they had a habit of doing this to other people who they weren't getting along with. "I'll put a stop to this once and for all," I thought. After all, the police won't look for a suspect long. They would think it was drug related! I would be helping the police out! They won't ever suspect me! I've never been in trouble, never done drugs, nothing that would cause someone to link me to this, so I would never be suspected!"

Now, in this writing, I am allowing you to understand my mindset after I watched the video. I was allowing the enemy to deceive me into thinking that I needed to handle the problem myself. That is the enemy's lies. He will deceive us into doing things, making us believe that we can get away with it. But God knows all things and will bring light to the darkness. No matter our motives, there are consequences that will follow. Yet, at this time, I thought I could get away with it, easily at that, because of the circumstances involved. Still going to church, and knowing I loved the Lord, people knew nothing of the real feelings I was fighting inside. No one knew anything, but me, the enemy, and the Lord! I had this intense tug of war between good and evil going on inside of me. The more it tugged at me, the more my mind played out the "perfect scenario." I was sucked in until I started seeing what my future would look like if I followed through... prison! I began to imagine my life without my family, and better yet, how could I help protect Hannah at all if I was put away, because these weren't the only ones she was vulnerable to.

I had started running 5 miles a day, along with going to the gym, trying to get myself together, and release some of this energy that was building up in me to do the unthinkable! I began to break inside, like a shattered mirror as I looked at myself as God started dealing with my heart! I began to cry uncontrollably. There was a breaking in my heart, yet I was clinching my fist so tight and gritting my teeth so hard trying to fight my feelings. I was breaking down emotionally. During this time, I was praying and begging God to take this out of me! I was crying out, "Lord! Please help me get control of myself! I told Him what my plan was, as if He didn't know my thoughts and intentions. I told Him if He didn't help me I was going to execute those plans, and I didn't want to do that! I wept bitterly! "HELP! I don't have the strength to overcome this on my own!" I knew my life, along with my family, those girls' families and friends would be devasted! Even worse, since those girls didn't know the Lord, I WOULD HAVE INNOCENT BLOOD ON MY HANDS! Death is not my decision! I cried out with agonizing deep emotions that felt like my guts were coming out! Then, one day as I was running, I heard the Lord say,

> *"If you only love them which love you, what reward do ye have?" (Matthew 5:46 KJV)*

I stopped in my tracks! I knew where this was headed… *"LOVE YOUR ENEMIES! (Matthew 5:44) KJV*

I could hear him saying, *"Hatred stirreth up strifes: but love covereth all sins. Proverbs 10:12 (KJV)*

Then I began visualizing Jesus hanging on the cross, while being mocked and ridiculed, after the near death scourging he endured to the point that his visage was marred insomuch that he didn't even look human! As he then carried that heavy weight of a cross on his weakened back up the hill to the place called Golgotha, or the skull, to be nailed down to his cross, WILLINGLY, I might add, then to be suspended high into the air, exposed in the most humiliating way, while they laughed and mocked him, "Come down, why don't you save yourself, if you really be God!" It was just pure humiliation in the highest form. But he NEVER ONCE tried to save himself, not one time, not to prove he really was God, not to say, "HERE, I'LL SHOW YOU WHO I AM!" Not to give the world any evidence that he truly did have all power at the sound of him calling on 12 legions of angels to take him out of his misery! NO! Not for one minute! You see, he knew the plan from the beginning, he knew the reward he would gain to go through it and not allow the sound of distraction take him off of his purpose and destiny he was sent here on earth to do. Which was to save mankind. He was so focused on that plan, that as he looked out among those who mocked and ridiculed him, beat and scourged him, because they had accused him of blaspheming God, wrongly accused him, because of their perception of him, that would cause them to hate him literally to death! THEN, I HEARD IT LOUD AND CLEAR! As I could see this scene in my head, I completely forgot about the situation with my daughter and the girls who jumped her, I heard him say, "FATHER FOR-GIVE THEM, FOR THEY KNOW NOT WHAT THEY DO!" It was such a chilling moment, I stopped in my tracks as I felt so ashamed. I'm almost sure it was how Peter felt when he denied our Lord those three times, just after he told Jesus he would never deny him. He said he would go to the end with him, yet he did the very thing he thought he could never do to the Lord he loved so much, all because of the pressure! I knew exactly how he had to have felt! Oh my, to have such a tangible touch of the pureness of our Father's love was beyond express-ing! As he was delivering me from myself, I sobbed right there on the train tracks so hard, my nose was pouring buckets! I couldn't breathe through my nose, and I even thought about that! It is God who breathes life into us, who are we to decide when to take that gift of life away!

Behold, for peace I had great bitterness: but thou hast in love to my soul delivered it from the pit of corruption: for thou hast cast all my sins behind thy back. **Isaiah 38:17 (KJV)**

OH MY! This was an awakening moment for me, but it made me free! I began to ask the Lord to help me forgive them. I told him I really want to, but to just say I did wasn't enough, because to think about them still brought anger to my soul! I prayed and prayed for the Lord to help me, and he said, "The more you pray for them, the more free you will become," It was the same lesson as he taught me years ago after my divorce. I started to pray for them, and then one day, I even caught myself saying to the Lord, "OK, Lord, I know you said pray for them, but I'm asking you to please let me be the one to witness to them about your love someday!" I knew then, I was free!! It was a sincere request, and thus far, I have witnessed to one who held her down, the one I was fueled over the most! We were able to discuss this one day through texting and she apologized sincerely to me. I talked to her about God's love and told her how much He loves her, and even told her that I loved them both. The other girl is in prison at this writing, but I am believing God will honor my request and I will eventually get the chance to witness to her about God's amazing love as well! He has proven time and time again that His LOVE NEVER FAILS!

People so often will get into this saying and get stuck, "I will forgive but I won't forget. I'll love them from a distance." That is part fact, we as humans have a memory recall, subconscious, in our brain that stores up information, good or bad. We remember occasions or events that automatically come to the frontline of our thinking when something familiar comes to us to remind us of a particular situation from the past. So it's hard to forget things that brought such impact to our lives especially when it was a traumatic event causing emotional damage, that led to bitterness, depression, anxieties, isolation, seclusion, loneliness, suicidal thoughts, etc. All those negative emotions we tend to carry around in our hearts eventually show up at a much later time in our lives, completely stripping us of any abundant life that Jesus died for us to richly enjoy! But forgetting and forgiveness are two totally different things, forgiveness is an act of the true essence of love, and love bears no record of wrong. WHY? Because God is love and He forgives and casts it in the sea to be remembered no more! It's no coincidence that He says forgive, that you may be forgiven, in Mark 11:25 & 26, because Jesus shed his blood for us to be forgiven from our sins! Therefore, we are to forgive as He has forgiven!

Forbearing one another, and forgiving one another, if any ,am have a quarrel against any: even as Christ forgave you, so also do ye.
Colossians 3:13 (KJV)

Just before he gave up the ghost (died), he had to ask for the forgiveness of mankind sins, being that he was standing in the gap for us. He became the propitiation for our sins, was required to release us from our debts, so to speak, through this act of shedding his blood to receive the forgiveness required because he loved us. We in turn are required to do the same, we are required to love and forgive in order to be released of bondage. When we say we have love but truly haven't forgiven, it tends to show up later through mental and physical

77

behaviors. Lastly, to love from a distance is sometimes required, depending on the actions and behaviors that others exhibit around you, if you feel threatened by an individual or tempted to do what you know is not right to do, in order to stay focused on what God has for your life, then you may love them from a distance.

It was then that the Lord showed me two visions, that forever changed my thinking about the addicts.

Vision number 1: I saw a quick vision of a bunch of cockroaches, it was dim to dark light, they were moving around (I almost got sick at that) but then a light came on and they frantically began to run for cover! They all went different ways looking for a place to hide! Once in a while you would see one come out in the light, as if he were looking for food or something to take back to the nest but was hesitant to stay out. It was like he was nervous or something, as if he would be seen or noticed. And that's when the Lord spoke and said, this is their character. This is how they act because of shame, guilt, embarrassment, and fear of being rejected. This is how they perceive themselves, because they know how people talk about them and react to them. They are treated in this day almost the same as the lepers were in the bible. The majority are homeless or live in nasty housing because of a lack of desire and are only brave enough to come out among others to get what they need to feed their addictions. But they usually are loyal to each other to help feed off each other in exchange for favors or other needs. It's just a survival mode to stay alive, but no thought of thriving, as their self-esteem and confidence is completely wiped out!

Vision number 2: The next vision was heart breaking. I saw a vision of the scene on Rudolph the Red-Nosed reindeer, where the little elf, (Hermey the dentist), Rudolph, and Cornelius went just before the storm came to misfit island. Rudolph was going to run away for being rejected by his parents, Santa, and the team due to his very unusual nose glowing and the embarrassment it would bring if they accepted him. They met all the misfits, who told they were misfits because they didn't turn out to be like the rest of the toys that were made. They had different defects that caused them to be REJECTED! Therefore they were all together on this little island called, "MISFIT IS-LAND." I saw where Rudolph told them he would go back and tell Santa to come and pick them up, that he was certain that there were many boys and girls who would love to have them. The misfits got really excited! The storm came after Rudolph, the elf, and Cornelius left to go tell Santa. The storm got worse and worse bringing much doubt and more disappointment to the misfits, as they waited on Santa to come. Thinking all hope was gone, they began crying and saying, well, maybe next year. While in the meantime, because of the storm that arose, it made room for Rudolph's gift to be used instead of rejected. His gift eventually benefitted them all, not just Rudolph. So, the despair was increasingly rising over at misfit island thinking that maybe Santa didn't want hand them out either. Just when things seemed hopeless, they heard the sound of the bells jingling in the air and began to see a red light coming through the air. They started screaming, "IT'S RUDOLPH! AND SANTA!" Then, after I saw all of this, the Lord spoke to me about the addicts and even those who are broken-hearted and rejected. He said, "this is how they feel inside. THEY JUST WANT SOMEONE TO LOVE THEM AND TO BE ACCEPTED!" I began to cry so hard! "I created mankind in my image and likeness, and I AM LOVE! It is vital to man's soul to know they are loved, and to feel that love regardless of circumstances in their lives."

> *Let all your things be done with charity. (love)* **1 Corinthians 16:14 (KJV)**

> *My little children, let us not love in word, neither in tongue; but in deed and in truth.* **1 John 3:18 (KJV)**

But remember, love is a fruit of the spirit and has no limitations or boundaries, and to say you love them, you would pray for them to be made free of the thing in which they are bound, so that God can reconcile that which has been broken in their life. That broken piece inside of them has caused them to stay bound, but He desires to mend those broken places so they can be reconciled back to Him. Also, in reaching out to love them by letting them know how much Jesus loves them, and if they have a need that we not overlook them as if they deserve what they are getting. Instead, let them know God has a plan and purpose for their lives. Sometimes just a little attention to let them know you love them, Jesus loves them, and you haven't written them off, goes farther than anything else does.

Let's reach out in love and show Jesus to the world!

Herein is our love made perfect, that we may have boldness in the day of judgement: because as he is, so are we in this world. There is no fear in love, but perfect love casteth out fear: because fear hath torment. He that feareth is not made perfect in love. We love him, because he first loved us. If a man say, I love God, and hateth his brother, he is a liar: for he that loveth not his brother whom he hath seen, how can he love God whom he hath not seen? And this commandment have we from him, That he who loveth God loveth his brother also. **1 John 4:17-21 (KJV)**

Chapter 10

Saving Grace

As I walked this journey with God leading me how to trust Him, I had put Hannah in God's hands again. I went to a Kenneth Copeland meeting in Columbia, SC for three days with my mother and few friends. On the last day of the conference I felt this strong urge to give a certain amount of money. Giving that amount would only leave me with enough money to pay my part of the gas and stop and eat at Cracker Barrel where they had all decided they were going to eat on our way home. I kind of argued with myself as to whether or not to put that in the plate (and no, I wasn't coached, forced, or condemned to do that, as a matter of fact they had not even mentioned offerings yet). When the offering plate came by, I hurried up and threw it in the plate so I wouldn't fight it anymore. It was kind of funny though because when it was over, they had a random drawing of everyone's names that came to the conference. Three names were picked, and I WON ONE!!! Boy, I was excited. Needless to say, what I received was awesome! But the GREATEST GIFT, was when we got home. I left in my car to go to my house and my mom called and said that Hannah was on her steps when she drove up. She asked if she could stay there. She wanted to be off of drugs and was ready to give her life back to God. It was a struggle as to let her stay, not knowing if she was just saying that because of not having anywhere to live or if she was truly serious. So, my mom said after talking with her she felt led to let her stay and see if she was truly wanting help or not. Hannah was so excited and was just bubbling! A short while later, she got a job at a restaurant and had gained some weight back. Her face had cleared up and she was doing great. Next we did a drug test, and it was negative after about a month which meant she could see her daughter again, which was my prayer also! Shortly after this, she changed jobs and worked for a catering company. She catered weddings and the Lord blessed her with a 2015 car, paid for!

Never give up on anyone who has fallen into deep dark places. God can and will save, deliver, make free, and restore if we will first love, then pray, believe and stand on His promises! Don't enable or contribute to their habits but give them to God completely and wholly! Trust that He knows how to get them out. Do what He says do, and He will bring it to pass! God is faithful to keep His promises! HIS LOVE NEVER FAILS!!

Chapter 11

Love Never Fails

The Spirit of the Lord is upon me, because he hath anointed me to preach the gospel to the poor; he hath sent me to heal the brokenhearted, to preach deliverance to the captives, and recovering of sight to the blind, to set at liberty them that are bruised. **Luke 4:18 (KJV)**

(vs.9) I am the door: by me if ANY man enter in, he shall be saved, and shall go in and out, and find pasture. (vs.10) The thief cometh not, but for to steal, and to kill, and to destroy: I am come that they might have life, and that they might have it more abundantly. **John 10:9-10 (KJV)**

*For God so loved the world, that he gave his only begotten Son, that whosoever believeth in him should not perish, but have everlasting life. -***John 3:16 (KJV)**

Here are some powerful testimonies that I pray will encourage you and help you see just how much Jesus loves you and if He will do it for these people, He WILL do it for you, or your loved ones!

For there is no respect of persons with God! **Romans 2:11 (KJV)**

TESTIMONIES

CHAD SISK

I am crucified with Christ: nevertheless I live; yet not I, but Christ liveth in me: and the life which I live in the flesh I live by the faith of the Son of God, who loved me, and gave himself for me. **Galatians 2:20 (KJV)**

It feels good being a child of God, washed in the blood of Jesus Christ, with a meaningful, purposeful life filled with joy, peace, and happiness. I must tell you that my life has not always been like this. I've always tried to tell what the Lord has done for me, but because I would get nervous, it wouldn't come out right. One night I was praying about my testimony, and the Lord told me to name it, "Just Trying to Fit In." That's all I ever wanted to do in life was to "fit in," to be accepted, liked, recognized, and successful. This is something I feel we all have in common. I'm going to tell you how to be all these things in Jesus, and not in the world. The scripture God gave me to back my testimony is Galatians 2:20. I'm ashamed of the life I was living before Jesus saved me. I'm going to share with you my childhood until now, to let you know that sin will take you farther than you want to go, and make you pay a price more than you are willing to pay.

I grew up in Gilkey, North Carolina, right on Cathey's Creek. I have two brothers and one sister. We were a poor family and had our problems, but we all loved each other. Dad worked a lot and wasn't home much; mom worked at Gilkey Service

Center to try and make ends meet. Sometimes we attended Gilkey Church of God with my mom and mama. I always wanted to be like my dad. I loved him so much growing up, but he was always in and out of trouble because of alcohol and drugs. I hated alcohol and drugs, seeing what it did to my family, and told myself that I'd never touch those things. Growing up was tough. I was a little overweight and we never really could afford nice clothes. On top of that, I was backwards, couldn't read or write very well, and that made it hard to make friends in school. All I wanted to do was "fit in."

At the age of seven I was at my mama's, and we were getting ready for bed. She had the television on, watching Jimmy Swaggart Crusade. He began to preach and the spirit of God began to deal with me in a mighty way. By the time he had made the altar call, I was in tears. Right before the altar call, Jimmy Swaggart stopped and said that the Spirit of God was telling him that a seven year boy was watching, and that was the night I needed to give my heart to the Lord. Without a doubt it was me! My heart was pounding out of my chest, and I was crying my eyes out. Jimmy also said that God was telling him that whoever it was would go through many things in life, but would use it to do the work of God. Little did I know he was prophesying my life. I remember it well; I gave my heart to the Lord that night. I ran in the other room where mama was, told her what had just happened, and had her write a letter to Jimmy and tell him that was me he was talking about.

Even though I gave my heart to Jesus, I wasn't in church, and didn't have a Christian role model. It seems like I just faded back into the world. Somewhere around the age of nine, my mom and dad got divorced, and that was pretty painful. I really didn't understand what was going on. I just knew it broke my heart seeing my family separated, and not all of us together. Looking back, I realize that parents need to recognize they are not the only ones that pay during a separation or divorce. I know, firsthand, how much it hurts children.

In school, I started being the class clown, because that was the way I could be recognized. After all, I was just trying to "fit in." By the age of sixteen, I got a job at Stonecutter Mills, working second shift. I was tired of not having anything. I tried to go to school and hold down a job but ended up dropping out in the 11th grade. This proved to be one of the bigger mistakes I made as a young man. While working at Stonecutter, I met Melissa, the "love of my life." We soon married and had a son together. After working there a few years, I realized I wasn't getting anywhere working forty to forty-eight hours a week for a little over $200. I quit and opened a car detail shop and soon selling cars, making a lot more money and feeling like I had the world by the tail. Everything was going my way. For once in my life I felt like had finally "fit in." People were beginning to recognize me and like me. I had money, a new home, cars, and other material things. With all that came new friends. I began running and hanging with my new friends, who were known for messing with alcohol and drugs. The devil had begun painting a really good picture about the new crowd I was running with. They were popular, and, at that time, I thought "cool."

As much as I hated alcohol and drugs, because I had seen what it did to my family, I really wanted to just "fit in" with them. I began drinking and soon thereafter, I started doing meth, otherwise known as "crank." At first the drug made me feel like I was on top of the world. I didn't feel like I was taking it because I needed to, it was just fun. Soon I saw the money that could be made on drugs. I began selling small amounts; small quickly turned into very large amounts, and with all this came a sense of power. Everyone in the drug world was looking up to me. I was the man, and I liked it. But I knew, deep inside, it was wrong. I was lying to my wife about my new friends, money, and behavior, trying to hide it all behind my new car business. Soon it was lie after lie after lie, and the pressure was building quickly. I was taking large amounts of nerve pills (Xanax) and doing meth to stay numb to what was really going on in my life. I was totally out of control and becoming very violent. On two separate occasions I was arrested for assault with a deadly weapon with intent to kill and inflicting serious injury, on top of many other charges. I now had all law enforcement watching me day and night trying to catch me for the drugs and weapons. The world saw me as a tough guy, known for crime and drugs, but inside, I was hurting and sin-sick in a bad way. I got shot, stabbed, and was involved in a number of bad car wrecks, where the guys that were with me had to be rushed to Winston-Salem Trauma Hospital, with broken backs and head injuries. I was right at death's door, and the picture the devil had painted was not turning out so pretty. I was really putting a lot of strain on my marriage and my wife.

Through all this, because of God's grace and longsuffering, He permitted me to live. Melissa had always told me that life was not about money, homes, or cars, but I just didn't listen to her. So, she decided we would try church. She suggested we go to Fellowship Holiness Church with her co-worker, Sonya. I was ready, because I was ashamed of myself and on top of that, the Holy Ghost was working on me. The money didn't make me happy anymore, the drugs didn't get me high, and the fun of sin had run out. G.B. Brown preached right at me. I went to the altar that morning but did not repent. It wasn't long before I was right back into the same old things. I was staying gone for weeks at a time and began running around on Melissa with another woman I met in the drug life. Melissa was at the end of her rope and ready to leave. My life was in shambles; I was in and out of jail and running out of money quick for paying lawyers, and bonds, while trying to keep up a $1000 a day drug habit. I was completely out of control.

Finally, the crime and sin caught up with me, and I wound up in jail, where no amount of money could get me out. That was probably the best thing that happened to me, but I didn't think so. I couldn't get the drugs in my body, and I was in so much pain. I was very depressed. I finally realized that I was not "fitting in." The pretty picture had turned out very ugly. He (Satan) had me right where he wanted, and began telling me what a loser I was, how I had lost my wife and son, and how I had destroyed my reputation and business. Then the devil began telling me that I should end all this misery and pain by committing suicide by hanging myself in that jail cell. For over a week I wrestled with suicidal thoughts and was very close to following through with it. Death seemed like some sort of relief. Then one night, over the intercom, they called for chapel. This is the part I like! A black man came preaching Jesus and that He could save me from my sin. This turned out to be the best day of my life! That night I yielded to God's call, and asked Jesus to save me from all unrighteousness. That instant Jesus saved me and loosed the chains of sin! I knelt down a sinner, very deep in sin, and came up a child of God, feeling like a brand new man! That feeling was indescribable! It felt like a million pounds had been lifted off my life and God had created in me a clean heart as Psalm 51 says. Two to three weeks later, on December 29th, at New Life Second Chance Chapel, at a prison in Greensboro, North Carolina, I made an outward expression to the world of an inward experience, that I was dead to sin and had risen in Christ, by getting baptized. I was taking the first steps of my brand new life. Several months later I was released from prison; a brand new man with a bad reputation for drugs, violence, and crime. But over the last few years, God has given me the opportunity to walk through all that. Let me say just how good God has been to me. First, I'd like to thank God for his mercy, grace, and longsuffering. I thank Him for His son, Jesus Christ, who long before I got saved, dropped in my heart that He was tired of me sinning: either turn to Him or die. He has placed me in a good church, with a Holy Ghost-filled Pastor, and given me peace, joy, happiness, and a sound mind. He has blessed me with a business that is making good money, another home, a wife that loves the Lord, another son, and I have a relationship with my first son, and on top of that, He has filled me with His Spirit! Before I received the Holy Ghost, I was saved, but I didn't have any backbone about me. God has given me the opportunity to go back into prisons and testify of what He has done for me. The Lord has changed my walk, talk, my whole life. I don't "fit in" with the world anymore. I have finally found a place where I "fit in." I fit in with God's people, in the House of God! God has truly made something out of nothing! We have an awesome Almighty! A God that can take racial prejudices out of a man. After all, how could I dislike anyone because of their color? It was a black man who loved God enough to come to the prison I was in, who told me that Jesus loved me and could save me. Galatians 2:20 sums it all up. The devil paints a pretty picture about new friends in the world. They do things against God; against their parents. The devil doesn't tell you those people are hurting on the inside. He doesn't tell you that behind that smile is a person in misery and pain. He doesn't tell you that the picture he is painting is deceiving. I'm a "Flag-man for Jesus." I'm here to wave a flag to tell you not to go down that road. I've already been down that road and its name is Disappointment, Heartache, Addiction, and Misery. If you've already started down that road, turn around, because at the end is a steep cliff that lands straight in the pits of hell!

You might say, "Chad, I'll never do drugs or drink alcohol, or these things you did in your life." I'm telling you, if you don't stay in church and keep living for Jesus, then there's no telling what you will do! I never thought I'd do those things either. In fact, I hated them, but it started out little. Little things, like sneaking out of the house, or being on the phone when I wasn't supposed to. Disobedience. Disobeying my mom and dad. Then my rebellion waxed worse and worse. From experience, it pays to serve God. The only hope you have in life is in Jesus Christ. If you miss God, you've missed it all. I've shared my "pretty picture" of following after the many things I thought would help me "fit in;" the twenty-seven years that the devil stole from me. But I've also shared with you the joys I have had with Jesus Christ. How, as I stated in 1 John, that "if we confess our sin, He is faithful and just to forgive our sins and cleanse us from all unrighteousness."

TRACY OWENS

I'd like to start off by saying, I THANK GOD I am even here today to give this testimony! I grew up in a good family, with a mom and dad that loved me, an older brother and myself. I was taken to church all my childhood life and knew what was right and wrong. Yet, I experienced a traumatic event as a young child. I was between the age of 3 or 4 years old, when my mom and myself had come home from doing laundry at laundry mat. We came in the house and just as mom was putting up things, a black man came through the hallway and pointed a gun at my head and grabbed my momma. He told me to sit in the corner and not make a sound and not to move or he would kill my momma. Then he took my mother back to the bedroom and I was so afraid to move I just cried. What seemed like forever, but really was not long he left running out the back door because he thought he heard a car pull up. My momma came and grabbed me, and we left the house to get help.

For many years of my life, I never knew what really had happened to my mom, and I never asked, because I didn't want to know. So, the holding in all that resentment and unknowing fear and trauma led me later down a path that would affect my whole life, and many that I loved. In my early teenage years, I began to smoke cigarettes and later smoke marijuana. I also drank alcohol, which later lead to other drug use. Because of the event as a child I was very racist and didn't like black people all because of one person's actions. I began getting into trouble over and over again in school, until I was finally kicked out for good. At the beginning of my tenth grade year, the principle told me he didn't want me back in his school. So that left me more free time to get into more mischievousness.

In my later teens I met a girl that I started dating and later married and had two daughters with. I had a good job and a new home, but I still didn't feel complete. I was still trying to fill an empty void in my heart. It seemed like no matter how bad or how good I was, nothing was filling this emptiness, hollow place in my heart. I had a friend (so called friend) who introduced me to methamphetamines. He knew my personality, and nature. He knew that if I tried it I would like it. He said these very words, "I shouldn't let you try this, because I know you going to like it." So, of course, I was going to try it then, and one hit…. that's all it took to get me hooked! Yes, I have to say that it made me feel good, good enough that I chose it over everything else that I loved, my life for one, my wife, and children, my job, my home, my freedom and my family.

I really didn't think about God at that time. It was all about me and what I wanted, so I did things my way. My wife and I eventually separated, and she took the girls with her. Feeling the sense of rejection and fear again I began to do some crazy things causing her to be afraid of me due to my behavior. I started my own meth lab in my building and a friend at that time, helped me to make it. He was much better at making the batches perfect because I was color blind so he could get it almost perfect if you call it that. I had my own supply and stayed to myself a lot, doing many crafts. I was my own handyman, and got a lot done back then, but it still caused me to act out in behaviors that got me into a lot of trouble later and almost took my life! I would go to where my wife and children lived, and she was scared of me. One time, there was a guy at her house, and I pulled out a razor knife and cut him multiple times and threatened him. I told him that if he told it was me, I would kill him. I was high on meth then, and he got treated but never told on me and I never got caught.

Eventually I would have a restraining order against me from my wife and children. I wasn't able to see them and that really put the icing on the cake. It was my youngest daughter's birthday and I drove by their house and saw her outside, so I threw a coloring book and some crayons out the window and told her happy birthday. My wife at the time wasn't around but it wasn't long until the police came to pick me up for going against the restraining order. From there I had many in and out of jail experiences and drug charges. I ran from the police on foot for miles and blew out my knee. I also fled in a vehicle through an open field in a little Honda car. I later got charges for fleeing and alluding arrest. As I was on a downward spiral in drugs and mounting up my charges, I went to prison twice, jail multiple times, and have received multiple felony charges. But all this was brought to a halt the day I was faced with a choice of life or death, although I chose death, God saw things differently as many people were praying for me through this whole ordeal.

My mom and dad, my family, and my church family were all praying. As I explained what happened that day, it just goes to show the power of prayer and the most magnificent and unconditional love of God. He loves us all, regardless of where you are or what you are doing, right or wrong.

Here goes… I was high on meth that day. I was hurting so bad inside. I felt like a failure as a husband, a father, a person in general! A million voices in my mind were reminding me I was worthless and I was a failure, so I went to my mom and dad's and got my 270 deer hunting rifle, and bullets. My older brother saw me get it and he knew what I was thinking. I remember him saying, "Don't do it Tracy, it's not worth it." As I walked out the door not saying a word, I got into my jeep Cherokee and left. I loaded the gun going down the road, put it beside me, and I grabbed a piece of paper and a pen, started writing my suicide letter. As I was driving, all of a sudden, the gun went off and scared me so bad, I jumped and swerved! It blew a hole in the floorboard of my jeep, so I reloaded the gun, and finished my suicide note. I pulled up at my wife's house. Her and my children ran out of the house. The next thing I know is the police came. They evacuated the whole neighborhood that we were in. I was at a standoff with the police alone. I felt like it was my only option to get out of this misery I was in. I couldn't take another minute of this torture I was in. I was convinced in my head that I wasn't worth anyone's time, and everyone including my children would be better off without me in their lives.

I saw a policeman try to go around the back of the house, while they were trying to talk me down and have me put the rifle away. I had just gotten out of prison from a 10-month sentence, and I wasn't going back, or so I thought. Even if I had to die, I wasn't planning on going back. I put the barrel in my mouth (remember it was reloaded), and I saw a policeman come towards me slowly. He aimed a taser gun at me and shot it. He missed me. At that time, I was so scared of what I was about to do I just closed my eyes and pulled the trigger!!! CLICK!… NOTHING! The gun misfired. I'd shot this gun many times over the years and never had it ever misfired or jammed!

The police tackled me, arrested me and I went to jail, costing me another prison sentence of nearly a year. This also caused one of the policemen to be emotionally disturbed, I was later told. When sobering up and coming down from the high in jail, I promised my girls I would never do drugs again. That was in 2005, and I haven't touched that stuff since! While I was in prison the first time, I received my divorce papers from my wife, which I wasn't going to accept as if I had a choice. That is what brought me to the episode with the standoff. So, this go around of prison, I decided I was going to stay off of drugs and live my life and maybe get a relationship with my children back sometime soon. After I got out of prison in 2006, I went to church more. I went mainly to see my children who would come to church with my parents, but I hadn't truly turned my life over to the Lord. I met a woman (the author of this book), who was an old friend, and after a little over a year, we began to hang out and drink. I was drinking every day, and it got worse and worse, until I had a bad wreck and was charged with a DUI.

In 2010, I gave my life to the Lord. He has delivered me from drinking too! Praise God! I attend church regularly, and God has blessed me with my home. He gave back the home that I had purchased before I got into all the meth, and at this writing of this testimony it is paid in full! God has blessed me with an awesome good paying job, and a loving wife who has helped me see God's love is unconditional. I now have a better outlook on life! He has restored my relationships with my children, given me two more children (stepchildren), an awesome grand-daughter who adores me, and another grand baby on the way! Also have a friendship with my ex-wife, and she is no longer afraid of me, because that crazy person is NOT WHO I AM when I'm not on drugs! He delivered me of racism, as my wife asked me one day, "What if it would have been a white man that held that gun to your head and took your mother in a back room? Would you hate all white men?"

I replied, "I don't know. He wasn't white, so I can't answer that."

Then, she replied, "Well that was one person. He just happened to be a different color, but there are good and bad in every different race. One bad person shouldn't set your like or dislike to a whole race and take up precious opportunities with many others! That is the enemy stealing something God has planned later!"

All of the sudden God I felt conviction started crying and repented. He delivered me right then and there and healed me from hatred! I choose to love as JESUS loves! My wife called my momma and told her to talk to me about this. I found out some 30 years later, that he didn't rape her. He put a pillow over her face. She was praying under her breath, and he heard a car come down the road that was loud and ran. NOW, I am a brand-new person, headed in a completely new direction, not in drugs, but success, and not towards hell but HEAVEN! ALL THANKS TO THE GOOD LORD FOR HIS UNFAILING, UNCONDITIONAL, NEVER GIVING UP ON ME KIND OF LOVE!!! Praise God!!! Because He loved me, He saved me from the tormenting everlasting hell flames. He saved me to tell YOU, the person reading this testimony today, that He loves YOU as much as He does ME! I am GRATEFUL and pray this gives encouragement to the next struggling suicidal drug addicted felon! Don't wait, surrender it all to Him today!

JOHN BLACK

I just want to share my story of how I went from a drug addicted, porn addicted, abusive, low life person…a person that I hated, to the person sitting here today being able to hold my head up high, and praise God that all my sins are in the sea of forgetfulness. I will start by telling you the person I was, and how I became a born-again child of God. I was 14 years old when I was first introduced by a family member to alcohol and weed (marijuana). Then at the age of 16, I was introduced to Xanax, and not much older than 18 or 19 it escalated to crack cocaine, then methamphetamines and acid. You name it, I did it. Thank God, I was never introduced to heroin or angel dust, but I was already headed down the wrong road. I tried living my way for a lot of years, and the main drugs that kept dragging me down were opiates and meth. I am now 36 years old, but from the age of 16 to probably 31 years old, I worked and outside of working, which I never held down a job for long, I was not even thinking about the Lord, or the "big picture." My life revolved around drugs, and they dictated my life. I always had a conscience, thank God… and I always hurt and felt bad about my choices in life, but I couldn't control my addictions. If it wasn't both, it was opiates, that really drug me through hell for many years. I started really taking pain killers back around 2008, and you can say I was hooked right away, because it took away all my pain. I got a high from it that I really liked. I was in a car wreck in the early 2000's from being up for 5 days on methamphetamines. Of course, I shouldn't have been behind the wheel, but I was. I fell asleep and crossed the road and hit a culvert at 45mph, then immediately stopped by running into a power pole in the middle of someone's yard. I had a friend with me that could have easily lost his life, just as well as I could have, but the Lord was with us both, even then, when I didn't deserve His grace. We both crushed a disc in our lumbar spine, and I messed up my neck on a different occasion fighting with my brother. These injuries are why pain killers had become attractive to me. They seemed to deal with the physical and mental pain I suffered. After I explain how I hit rock bottom, I will tell you how I came to know the Lord, Jesus Christ, as my personal Lord and Savior.

As you can already see, I had always mingled in some type of drugs. It was May of 2018 when I just about took my life and was admitted to the 5th floor (psychiatric unit) of the hospital for almost a month. My wife and I who were married September 7, 2014 at the church we attended. We'd been members for about a year, because we found out my wife was pregnant with my first daughter. We had another one come along less than two years later, so we tried getting our family in church, and get a real family going. But we let the devil get to us, and got out of church which eventually led to both of us being back on meth. We fought, split up, and our poor daughters were put in

DSS care at my mother's home. From there I lost all sense of reality. I continued abusing opiates, which I had a prescription for but of course I didn't take as prescribed. I would run out early, and I wouldn't be worth anything to anyone. I managed to stay off dope long enough to get my girls back, but my wife and I were split up and my wife was really bad out in the streets on dope. So, we fought over the children, over every little thing. I never believed for one minute we would be back together like we are today. Praise God! But going back to May of 2018, I was depressed, hated myself for not being able to provide for my 2 little girls, and for not having my wife and a relationship with the Lord. I just hated everything about myself. So, I went to my medicine bottles and I had planned on taking all the trazadone that I had. I should've had a whole bottle, but honest to God, to this day, there wasn't but like 2 or 3 in the bottle, and I didn't have anything else to OD on. I just went back to my room where I was staying at my mom's, because I had lost my home, I laid back down where I had been laying for 3 or 4 days, very depressed. But then this is when My Heavenly Father stepped in and said enough. I was taken to the 5th floor by my mother and was introduced to a doctor that I think helped save my life. I am on Social Security because I have a lot of health problems, mental problems, depression, bipolar, etc. But this doctor was very smart, and God sent. He helped me get on proper medications. Through behavioral health classes, and me asking the Lord to forgive me, putting God first, I am now less than a month shy of being sober and off opiates and meth for a year. Praise God! Of course, I had to get back in church as soon as I got out of the hospital and take things one day at a time. My wife and I agreed to take things slow, and attend church together, and now we both are sober and have our own place. We have a car that is paid off and attend church regularly. We owe it all to God. Once we put Him first in our lives again, and got serious about our walk with the Lord, He has more than blessed our home, and family. My wife works every day and we don't go without because the same God that saved us, delivered us, and restored our lives, is the same God that provides for us. I could never be more grateful for His grace and mercy and mostly His unconditional love.

ROBERT BLACK

My name is Robert Black, and this is my story. I spent 23 years bound by addiction, that ultimately resulted in me serving 5 prison terms. This is an overview of my addiction and how I beat it through Jesus Christ. I grew up in a split home, and those I was raised by were alcoholics. Many times, late night drinking turned into drunken brawls, so went my childhood. At the age of 8, I was introduced to my first drink of alcohol, and as unfortunate as that was it started a downward spiral. At the age of 13, another family member introduced me to marijuana. Then at the age of 15, I was introduced to the most destructive drug I have ever encountered, methamphetamines. Within the next few years, I started on what would become a vast criminal record, consisting of 38 total incarcerations. With time in the county jail, along with 5 prison terms, I had no respect for anyone. One of my felonies came after an all nightery of smoking cocaine, I stumbled upon the court District Attorney's home by accident, walked in and helped myself. Turned out that I was so high, I didn't realize I had already gone on a burglary spree, which had prompted the police to be on the lookout for a suspect on foot. Turns out alone I had committed 19 felony breaking and entering (B&E's), no resolution. This ends up being my life for the next 20 plus years. I joined the Aryan Brotherhood in prison and fought so many times I can't even remember. I've done some of the vilest inhumane things a person could even imagine. I've choked people out after they left the bank and taken every penny off them. I've done roughly 100 home invasions, cracked safes, and stole everything I could get my hands on. All these events, which are only a few to keep this testimony at reasonable length, cost me everything; my kids, my home, my 1st marriage, literally everything! Upon my last incarceration, I vividly remember looking in the mirror, a hollow-eyed shell of what I once was, and I said out loud, "YOU'RE A JUNKIE!" These words sounded in my chest like a beating drum and I wept uncontrollably. I vowed then and there to God that if He could take it from me, that I'd live the rest of my life for Him. The power of God came in that jail cell in RCDC, and I was baptized in the Holy Ghost and Fire not many days later. To this day, the fire of God is still burning just as strong as the day I received Him, and I've not been the same since! I've tried everything to break the chains of addiction and hate! Jesus broke every chain I ever had and today I'm living proof; God is alive and well! This is only a partial testimony of

The Saving Grace of Jesus and the Unfailing and Unconditional Love of the Father!

MELISSA BAUTISTA

Before I was ever even born, the devil tried to kill me as I later realized the enemy had my mom on the verge of an abortion, due to her feeling ashamed of the way she was living at the time. And ever since I see he has tried to take out, as I was an addict for 20 some odd years of my life. It started with cigarette smoking, then drinking, and ultimately heavy drugs that had a hold of me to the point of prostitution for the next fix. Being addicted led to me being in a drug house, high as I could be, hearing and seeing things (like demonic stuff) I was so scared of. I began to beg God to help me. Then one day God told me to get up and walk out and never look back. I did just that. He has since opened many doors for me. I live with my mom now and have my son who had been with my mom due to my decision to use drugs. I have a great supportive family. Since being delivered from drugs, I have enrolled in college and become a Dean's list student. Initially I was studying electrical engineering, but I just wanted to serve God, so I laid down that career. I enrolled into Valor Christian College where I am now currently a straight A student and working towards being an Evangelist. I have an amazing job where I make good money and am acknowledged for being one of the best on the team for one of the top dental insurance companies in the United States. God is awesome and I give Him all the glory, honor, and praise!

JUSTIN ROPER

I grew up in a small rural area of Rutherford County. To me at the time, I had a fairly normal life. Being raised by my grandparents, I was spoiled yet very secluded from the world. I did great in school. I attended church regularly and overall my childhood years was good, or so I thought. See, my addiction started long before I picked up that first drug as a teenager. I felt like an outsider and just wanted to fit in. Very soon after high school, I started seeing the world and the life of the streets. It got hold of me through drugs, then the money and the lifestyle followed. But hey, a kid of 18-19 gets shown more love in the streets than his own mom showed, it was hard not to live that life. At age 22, I injected my first drug. I just wanted to try it. I loved it. It numbed my pain and felt good. I had no more worries. In 2011, I had my first criminal charge, and shortly after, I had my first overdose. That wasn't enough to stop me. I was in and out of jail, homeless, hungry, and doing ANYTHING to get another fix. I didn't believe in God, because I didn't believe He would let me get so far gone. I just gave up. I was beat and raped, among other terrible things due to my choices. Heroin became my king and I was its servant. In 2016, my 4th heroin overdose happened, and I spent days on life support. The only thing I really remember is trying to scream for help, but it was dark, and no one could hear me scream! I remember Hannah was with me that night, and later her and her mother told me what happened. Hannah called her mother (who is a nurse, also the author of this book) because I overdosed, and Hannah said I wasn't breathing and was blue. She called her mother for help, because she panicked, and her first thought was to call her. Her mother asked if she had any Narcan. She hollered, "NO I DON'T HAVE ANY NARCAN!" Her mother said, "CALL 911!" She said, "MOMMA PRAY FOR JUSTIN, PLEASE!" She called for help on my phone while she put her phone up to my ear and her mother prayed and called life into my body. I don't remember anything, as I myself, only remember going through this long pitch-black tunnel. There is no darkness here on this earth to ever describe just how dark it was. It was also eerily cold, and I was screaming for help inside but wasn't able to physically voice it outwardly. It was as if I no longer had use of my physical body and mouth to speak through, so no one could hear my plea for help. But God! After this, I just remember waking up in the hospital. I now believe I was going to hell, but God saved me and gave me another chance at life which I am grateful for. When I woke up, I turned my life over to God and begged Him to take the desire to use drugs away from me. After 6 arrests, going in and out of detox, I decided I didn't want to live that life any longer. Today, I am clean and have an amazing woman that I am engaged to and two amazing kids that mean the world to me. I fight hard to stay clean and with God in my life and my relationship with Him, I do one day at a time. If I can do it, the next addict can do it. Please ask for help and pray to God because HE truly saved my life, and He will save anyone who calls on Him.

CHELSEA CHAMBERLAIN

I am a grateful servant in long-term Recovery. I am a wife, mother, daughter, sister, aunt, friend, and productive member of society. My husband and I have 5 children, 2 businesses, we are proud homeowners, and we have a ministry faith based non-profit transitional housing for men wanting to recover from substance use, prison re-entry and homeless shelter. I am a peer support specialist. I am an artist and singer/songwriter. I have a great passion hope also through song. My substance use counselor told me 14 years ago, if I would stop using, I could write the rest of my story, it's a beautiful thing! I struggled in substance use for 21 years. I was also diagnosed at the age of 11 with bipolar disorder which affected me in all areas of my life. I was in and out of psychiatric hospitals, children's homes. I felt rejected, abandoned, and unloved like something was wrong with me. I was also diagnosed with PTSD and ADHD and was put on more medicines and became dependent on those medications as well and got a DUI. I received pain medication for injury, and then became dependent to them, as well as marijuana on a daily basis and alcohol. I knew I was facing my biggest challenge when my kids were taken from me. No one trusted me anymore and I wasn't allowed at my family gatherings or even at my mom's house. I felt my worst at this point because my kids were taken away from me for 14 months! I cried out to God and asked Him to deliver me from it all. I wanted to stop using for a long time. I could not stop on my own, but when I truly surrendered to God, withholding nothing back, and wanting His will for my life, He delivered me. Since 2016, I have been completely sober! Because of the strengths that I have developed along my journey, I am now a warrior! I am a recovery warrior, a prayer warrior, and a praise warrior! To remain engaged in my recovery I stay spiritually tuned up by meditating on God's word and in prayer. I continue to attend weekly recovery meetings. I have a strong support network. What motivates me to stay sober is enjoying the abundant life with my friends and family which I was once separated from. I am also motivated by being part of the solution and not the problem. I want to help as many people as possible, because with God and each other, WE DO RECOVER!

I pray that these real-life testimonies encourage others and allows everyone, regardless of their struggles, to see that you have never gone so far that God cannot help you! You are never a hopeless situation!

> *Behold, the Lord's hand is not shortened, that it cannot save; neither his ear heavy, that it cannot hear.* **Isaiah 59:1 (KJV)**

MAY THE GOD OF LOVE FILL YOUR HEARTS AND HOMES TODAY!

INVITATION

I would like to invite you to meet the LOVE that is described in this book, his name is Jesus, that you too, may be able to have your own experience of peace, joy, happiness, and comfort, and most importantly a life changing experience that will be lead you into his awesome presence for eternity! (heaven is real and so is hell, he loves you so much he made a way for you to live an abundant life in his love) If you would like to receive him as your own personal savior, this is what the bible says:

> *That if thou shalt confess with thy mouth the Lord Jesus, and shalt believe in thine heart that God hath raised him from the dead, thou shalt be saved. For with the heart man believeth unto righteousness; and with the mouth confession is made unto salvation.* **Romans 10:9-10 KJV**

> *For whosoever shall call upon the name of the Lord shall be saved.* **Romans 10:13 KJV**

The door of the greatest opportunity you will ever be offered is open to you right now, this minute Jesus is calling you, He loves you! Just answer His calling! Say yes to Him today, and meet the greatest love ever… the love that never fails!

My prayer and sole purpose of this writing and publication is that you, the one reading this very letter, would come to know and experience a love that is out of this world. Now let us together spread this love and let it be in Earth as it is in Heaven! Lord, touch the hearts now. Draw each one by your precious

Holy Spirit. Lord, I ask you now for a super abundant harvest of souls saved, delivered, hearts healed, and families and children restored by the power of Your spirit! All glory belongs to Jesus Christ, our Lord and Savior. I marvel at all you will and are doing through this very book you have inspired me to write. Thank you, Lord, for everyone you will save and change! To God be the glory for the great things He has done!

God bless you all!

About the Author

Author Crystal Owens lives in a small town in North Carolina. She is a devoted wife to her husband Tracy Owens of 9 years, a loving mother to two children and two stepchildren, and the grandmother (Mawmaw) of two beautiful granddaughters. She has been a nurse for 24 years and is currently still in the active field. Crystal is a devout Christian for years, which is the foundation of her passion to spread the true, unconditional love of God, sharing hope to all humanity after she experienced the unthinkable. Seeing her daughter struggle with a terrible drug addiction which she had no control over was the start of a new journey for Crystal. God led her through the horrendous emotional pain that left her feeling like a broken, helpless mom. Crystal turned her pain over to God as she felt she was literally dying inside. Through being completely transparent to the Lord regarding all her feelings, reading His word, listening to His instructions, and focusing on His ways, she saw God prove His faithfulness as her daughter overcame the addiction that held her captive. Now she is focusing on seeing the hurting healed, the broken mended, the tormented at peace, and the rejected accepted, as she too, had to learn how to love beyond feelings of hurt, pain, anger, frustration, disappointment, evil thoughts and bitterness through forgiveness. Now she is eager to teach those who struggle with emotional pain and unforgiveness about a love that prevails, it NEVER FAILS! And it's no love like you will EVER know until you experience for yourself! It is 100 percent guaranteed! It's God's love!

CPSIA information can be obtained
at www.ICGtesting.com
Printed in the USA
BVHW082319260921
617440BV00001B/63

9 781733 805131